NATIONS
OF THE WORLD

JAPAN

Jen Green

RAINTREE
STECK-VAUGHN
PUBLISHERS

A Harcourt Company

Austin   New York
www.steck-vaughn.com

Steck-Vaughn Company

First published 2001 by Raintree Steck-Vaughn Publishers,
an imprint of Steck-Vaughn Company.
Copyright © 2001 Brown Partworks Limited.

Library of Congress Cataloging-in-Publication Data

Green, Jen
   Japan / Jen Green
      p. cm. — (Nations of the World)
   Includes bibliographical references and index.
   Summary: Examines the land, people, and history of Japan and discusses its current state of affairs and place in the world today.
      ISBN 0-8172-5783-7
      1. Japan—Juvenile literature. [1. Japan] I. Title. II. Nations of the World (Austin, Tex.)

DS806 . G68 2000
952--dc21   99-086751
                                                                  CIP

Printed and bound in the United States
2 3 4 5 6 7 8 9 0 BNG 05 04 03 02

Brown Partworks Limited
Project Editor: Robert Anderson
Designer: Joan Curtis
Cartographers: William Le Bihan and
   Colin Woodman
Picture Researcher: Brenda Clynch
Editorial Assistant: Roland Ellis
Indexer: Kay Ollerenshaw

Raintree Steck-Vaughn
Publishing Director: Walter Kossmann
Art Director: Max Brinkmann
Editor: Shirley Shalit

Front cover: snowcapped Mount Fuji and a blossom tree (background); Shinto priest adjusts the cermonial robes of a young man (left); *kanji* representing *Nippon*, the Japanese name for Japan (top left)
Title page: wood-block print of Mount Fuji by Katsushika Hokusai

Contents

Foreword

Since ancient times people have gathered together in communities where they could share and trade resources and strive to build a safe and happy environment. Gradually, as populations grew and societies became more complex, communities expanded to become nations—groups of people who felt sufficiently bound by a common heritage to work together for a shared future.

Land has usually played an important role in defining a nation. People have a natural affection for the landscape in which they grew up. They are proud of its natural beauties—the mountains, rivers, and forests—and of the towns and cities that flourish there. People are proud, too, of their nation's history—the shared struggles and achievements that have shaped the way they live today.

Religion, culture, race, and lifestyle, too, have sometimes played a role in fostering a nation's identity. Often, though, a nation includes people of different races, beliefs, and customs. Many have come from distant countries, and some want to preserve their traditional lifestyles. Nations have rarely been fixed, unchanging things, either territorially or racially. Throughout history, borders have altered, often under the pressure of war, and people have migrated across the globe in search of a new life or of new land or because they are fleeing from oppression or disaster. The world's nations are still changing today: Some nations are breaking up and new nations are forming.

As an island nation, Japan has been able to maintain a stable identity for many centuries, building a rich culture of great originality. Despite its isolation, however, Japan has been able to absorb cultural influences from overseas—from China, Korea, and most recently from the West—without losing sight of its own traditions. In the early 20th century, like many other nations, Japan went through a period of extreme nationalism, during which its rulers attempted to create a vast Japanese empire in the Pacific. Today, though, Japan is a stable democracy, whose constitution explicitly forbids military aggression.

Introduction

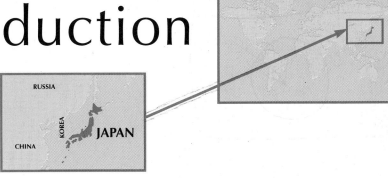

Yōkoso—"welcome" to Japan, a land where ancient and modern meet to make a unique culture. Modern Japan is one of the world's most advanced and wealthy nations. Despite its small size, its economy ranks in the world's top three in terms of its gross national product (GNP), along with those of the United States and Germany. Today Japan is best known for high-quality, high-tech goods, such as cars, computers, cameras, and televisions—products that are assembled partly by robots in up-to-the-minute, modern factories.

Yet Japan is also a land where ancient religions and traditions are part of everyday life. Businessmen throng the streets in suits on weekdays, but put on *kimono*—traditional robes tied with a sash—for festivals and holidays. In bustling cities gleaming skyscrapers tower over historic shrines and temples. Out in the country, high-speed "bullet" trains race past a patchwork of golden rice (paddy) fields.

The country of Japan is made up of a chain of islands in the Pacific Ocean, off the east coast of continental Asia. There are four main islands and thousands of smaller ones. From the coast the land rises steeply to jagged mountain ranges with forest-covered slopes and snowy peaks. Japan is a land of great scenic beauty, with steaming hot springs, glittering lakes, and thundering waterfalls. With frequent earthquakes, seasonal typhoons,

Snow-capped Mount Fuji is one of Japan's most famous sights. The Japanese consider the mountain a holy place and a powerful symbol of their country.

FACT FILE

- With a land area of 145,835 square miles (377,800 sq. km), Japan is smaller than California. Yet this small country has the seventh-largest population in the world.

- Japan is one of the most ethnically uniform nations in the world. Less than 1 percent of the population are of non-Japanese origin.

- Japan has a very low crime rate, with crime figures about one-eighth of the total in the United States.

- In Japan surnames (family names) come first, then given names.

The Japanese flag shows a red circle, symbolizing the sun, on a white background.

Everywhere you go in Japan, you will see these kanji, or characters (right). They represent Nippon or Nihon— the Japanese name for the country.

Japanese bills usually bear portraits of a famous author, scholar, or emperor as well as traditional symbols, such as Mount Fuji.

or tropical hurricanes, and the occasional volcanic eruption, the country has more than its fair share of natural drama.

In the early years of its history, Japan was greatly influenced by its neighbors, Korea and, particularly, China. The traditional Japanese style of government, writing system, arts, and architecture all owe much to ancient Chinese culture. About 150 years ago, however, Japan began to modernize rapidly, looking to Europe and the United States for inspiration. Today Japanese culture is a unique blend of East and West. Downtown restaurants serve hamburgers and pizzas as well as traditional dishes of fish and rice. Baseball and golf are popular national sports, as well as *sumo* (Japanese wrestling) and traditional martial arts.

The Japanese call their country Nippon or Nihon, meaning "source of the sun," because it is so far east. The English name "Japan" is probably a European version of a Chinese word meaning "land of the rising sun."

Japan's currency is the yen, which is written ¥. There are 1, 5, 10, 50, 100 and 500-yen coins (two of which— the 5 and 500-yen coins—have a hole in the middle) and 1,000, 5,000, and 10,000-yen notes. Because Japan has such a low crime rate, the Japanese usually use cash and use credit cards only occasionally.

Japan is a parliamentary democracy. Like Britain's king or queen, the Japanese head of state—the emperor—has no real power. Japan's national flower, the chrysanthemum, is also the emperor's symbol.

POPULATION DENSITY

Japan is one of the most densely populated nations in the world. Most towns and cities are found along the coastal plains of the country's larger islands. Many cities have grown so big that they form a huge urban sprawl or conurbation. By contrast, the mountainous areas inland are only sparsely populated and are havens for Japan's wildlife and plants.

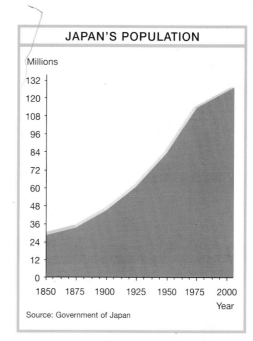

PERSONS

Per sq. mi	Per sq. km
130	50
520	200
1,810	700
5,200	2,000

TOKYO

Japan's population has risen steeply in the last 150 years.

PEOPLE AND POPULATION

Japan has a population of more than 125 million people. Its small land area means that it is one of the most crowded nations in the world. On average there are 860 people to each square mile (332 people per sq. km). This compares with only 26 people per square mile (10 people per sq. km) in the United States.

Japan's population is not evenly spread throughout the country, however. Most people live on narrow coastal plains, which are among the most

JAPAN'S POPULATION

Millions

132 — 120 — 108 — 96 — 84 — 72 — 60 — 48 — 36 — 24 — 12 — 0

1850 1875 1900 1925 1950 1975 2000

Year

Source: Government of Japan

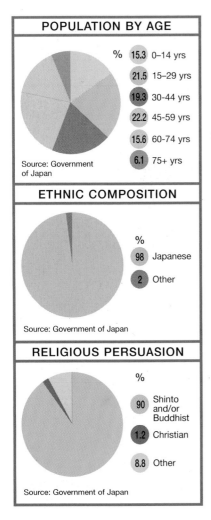

POPULATION BY AGE

%	
15.3	0–14 yrs
21.5	15–29 yrs
19.3	30-44 yrs
22.2	45-59 yrs
15.6	60-74 yrs
6.1	75+ yrs

Source: Government of Japan

ETHNIC COMPOSITION

%	
98	Japanese
2	Other

Source: Government of Japan

RELIGIOUS PERSUASION

%	
90	Shinto and/or Buddhist
1.2	Christian
8.8	Other

Source: Government of Japan

The charts above show how the Japanese population divides by age, ethnicity, and religion.

densely populated areas in the world. More than three-quarters of Japanese people live in towns and cities, leaving less than a quarter in the countryside. Japan's capital, Tokyo, is home to more than eight million people. The three next-largest cities— Yokohama, Ōsaka and Nagoya—each have more than two million people.

Japan's population is overwhelmingly Japanese—98 percent. Koreans make up most of the remainder (0.6 percent), with Chinese forming 0.2 percent. These people are largely immigrants who have come to Japan to find work or new opportunities. A people called the Ainu are thought to be some of Japan's earliest inhabitants, but today there are only some 14,000 Ainu left in Japan. Intermarriage between the Japanese and the Ainu is common, and experts calculate that as few as 200 people are pure-blooded Ainu people. The vast majority of this ancient and dwindling people live on the island of Hokkaidō in the north of Japan.

The Japanese are the longest-lived people in the world, with women expecting to reach the age of 82, and men 76. Today 16 percent of Japan's population are over the age of 60, with a relatively low figure, 15.3 percent, under the age of 14. This aging population (*see* p. 119) worries the Japanese government, who are concerned that the economy will be unable to support a large nonworking older population.

This chart shows that the Japanese population is overwhelmingly urban.

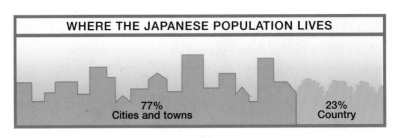

WHERE THE JAPANESE POPULATION LIVES

77% Cities and towns

23% Country

LANGUAGE AND RELIGION

Japan's official language, Japanese, has many local dialects (forms). The standard spoken dialect is that of Tokyo. The traditional Japanese system of writing is based not on an alphabet but on characters called *kanji*. There are several thousand *kanji*, each representing a different word. The *kanji* were originally based on Chinese characters. Over the centuries, however, they have come to look very different from their Chinese ancestors (*see* p. 108).

The main religions of Japan are Shinto and Buddhism. Shinto, which means "the way of the gods," is a very ancient faith. Buddhism, too, was introduced more than 1,500 years ago. In Japan, 90 percent of the population follow Shinto, and 75 percent are Buddhists. Most people follow both religions, and Buddhist temples are often found close to Shinto shrines. Christians make up just over 1 percent of the population. In addition, there are a variety of new religions that often blend elements from older religions and beliefs.

The National Anthem

The national anthem is called "Kimigayo," which means "Our Emperor's Reign." The words of the anthem are taken from a 1,000-year-old poem and were set to music in 1880 to celebrate the birthday of Emperor Meiji. The composer, Hiromori Hayashi, was a musician at the emperor's court. The song became Japan's national anthem in 1888.

Ten thousand years of happy
reign be yours.
Rule on, my lord, till what are
pebbles now
By ages united to mighty rocks
shall grow
On whose venerable sides the

How Japanese Is Written in This Book

Modern Japanese is sometimes written using the Roman alphabet, called *romaji* in Japanese. Most of the *romaji* letters used to represent Japanese sounds are pronounced much as they are in English. A few have a special pronunciation:

f	pronounced while pursing the lips
l	pronounced more like *r*
g	pronounced like *g* in "gate" at the beginning of a word but like *ng* in the middle.

Some vowels, too, are "long"; that is, the sound is held twice as long as a normal vowel. A long vowel is indicated by a bar (macron) over the letter—for example, a long *o* is written as ō.

Land and Cities

"The extreme part of the known world unto us is the noble island Japan...This country is hilly and pestered with snow."

A 16th-century Englishman's description of Japan

Japan is an island nation in the North Pacific Ocean, situated about 310 miles (500 km) off the mainland of Asia. To the west, across the Sea of Japan, lie the Russian Federation, China, and Korea. To the east lie the vast waters of the Pacific Ocean, with Canada and the United States some 4,500 miles (7,200 km) away.

There are four main islands. Farthest north is Hokkaidō, of which the northern tip is separated from the Russian island of Sakhalin by a narrow strait. To the south of Hokkaido is Honshū, which is by far the largest island. Two other large islands, Shikoku and Kyushū, lie southwest of Honshū, across the Inland Sea.

Together the four main islands make up an arc that curves through more than 15 degrees of latitude, from 30°N to 45°N—the distance between Maine and the Gulf of Mexico. In addition to the four main islands, there are some 3,900 smaller ones. Two island groups, the Rykūyū and the Bonin islands, dot the ocean to the south of the large islands.

The greatest distance from west to east in Japan is less than 200 miles (320 km), but from north to the south, the country stretches 1,400 miles (2,250 km). The great distance from north to south means the scenery and climate of Japan vary dramatically, from frozen wastes and ice floes in the north to tropical islands and coral reefs in the south.

Tokyo's Imperial Palace can be visited only on two days of the year. The rest of the year, the palace can be glimpsed from the Nijū-bashi Bridge.

FACT FILE

● Cities that stand at a comparable latitude to Japan's most southerly and northerly points are Miami and Montréal.

● Japan stands in one of the Earth's most volcanic zones, with some 65 active volcanoes. The country also lies in the West Pacific earthquake belt and has suffered many devastating shocks, notably in 1923 and 1995.

● Japan's rugged coastline measures an astonishing 18,500 miles (29,800 km).

● Tokyo has colder average January temperatures than Reykjavík, the capital of Iceland.

A huge plume of ash erupts from the summit of Mount Sakura-jima, in Kyūshū.

The Japanese believe that mountains are sacred places, and volcanoes such as Mount Fuji have long been worshipped for their power.

THE TERRAIN

The islands of Japan are really the tops of a great range of undersea mountains that rise from the floor of the Pacific Ocean. At one time Japan was connected to mainland Asia. At the end of the last Ice Age, some 10,000 years ago, the sea level rose and formed the Sea of Japan that today separates Japan from China.

Some 80 percent of Japan is mountainous. The mountains are covered with forests and dotted with sparkling lakes. Swift-flowing rivers cut through the ranges, forming craggy gorges. From the high ground inland, short, fast-flowing rivers tumble down to the sea.

A Land of Volcanoes

Many of Japan's mountains are volcanoes, including Mount Fuji (*see* p. 21), the country's highest point at 12,388 feet (3,776 m). There are more than 180 volcanoes, 65 of which are still active. Mount Sakura-jima,

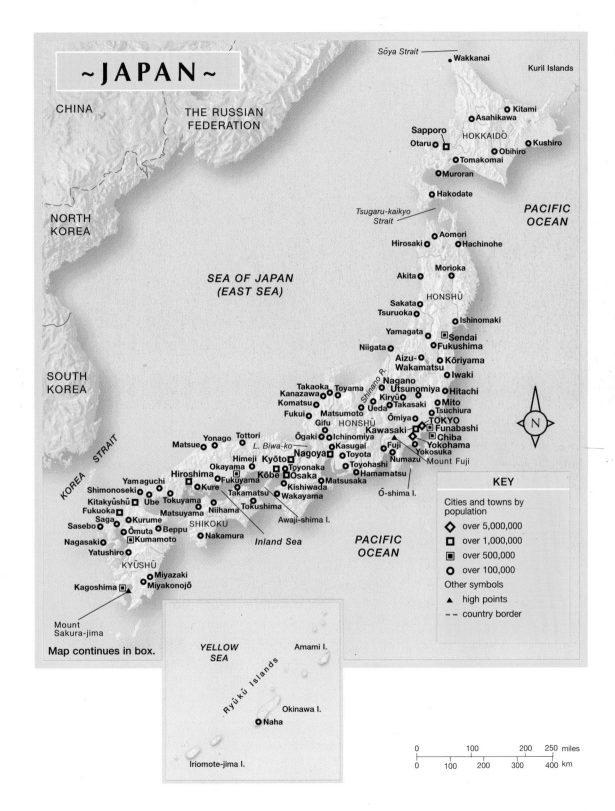

~JAPAN~

CHINA

THE RUSSIAN
FEDERATION

NORTH
KOREA

SOUTH
KOREA

SEA OF JAPAN
(EAST SEA)

Sōya Strait

● Wakkanai

Kuril Islands

● Kitami

● Asahikawa

Sapporo
● HOKKAIDŌ
Otaru ●□

● Kushiro

● Obihiro
● Tomakomai

● Muroran

● Hakodate

*Tsugaru-kaikyo
Strait*

PACIFIC
OCEAN

● Aomori
Hirosaki ● ● Hachinohe

Morioka ●
Akita ●

HONSHŪ

Sakata ●
Tsuruoka ●

● Ishinomaki

Yamagata ●
Niigata ● ■ Sendai
● Fukushima

Aizu-● ● Kōriyama
Wakamatsu
● Iwaki

Takaoka ● Nagano
Kanazawa ● Toyama ● Utsunomiya ● Hitachi
Komatsu ● Kiryū ● Takasaki ● Mito
Fukui ● Matsumoto Ueda ● ● Tsuchiura
Gifu ● Ōmiya ●
HONSHŪ TOKYO
Ōgaki ● Ichinomiya Kawasaki ◆ Funabashi
Yonago ● Tottori Kasugai ● ◆ Chiba
Matsue ● L. Biwa-ko Nagoya ● Fuji ● Yokohama
Himeji Kyōto □ Toyota ● Yokosuka
Okayama ● Toyonaka Numazu Mount Fuji
Hiroshima ● ■ Fukuyama Kōbe □ □ Osaka Toyohashi ●
Yamaguchi ● Kure ● Kishiwada Hamamatsu ●
Shimonoseki ● Takamatsu ● Wakayama Matsusaka ●
Kitakyūshū □ Ube ● Tokuyama ● Niihama Ō-shima I.
Fukuoka □ Matsuyama ● Tokushima
Saga ● Kurume ● SHIKOKU Awaji-shima I.
Sasebo ● Ōmuta ● Beppu ●
Nagasaki ● ■ Kumamoto ● Nakamura Inland Sea PACIFIC
Yatushiro ● OCEAN

KYŪSHŪ
● Miyazaki
Kagoshima ■ ● Miyakonojō

KOREA STRAIT

Shinano R.

Mount
Sakura-jima

Map continues in box.

Map continues in box.

KEY

Cities and towns by
population

◆ over 5,000,000
□ over 1,000,000
■ over 500,000
● over 100,000

Other symbols

▲ high points
-- country border

N

YELLOW
SEA

Amami I.

Ryūkū Islands

Okinawa I.

● Naha

Iriomote-jima I.

| 0 | 100 | 200 | 250 | miles |
| 0 | 100 | 200 | 300 | 400 | km |

and part of the crust was forced upward to form the craggy islands of Japan. The islands were further shaped by volcanoes, as molten rock from deep inside the Earth forced its way through weak points in the crust, to gush out to form landscapes of lava.

Today the tremendous forces that created Japan are still at work. The islands contain one-tenth of the world's active volcanoes, and from time to time, there is a major eruption. Japan's volcanoes do not erupt often, however. Earthquakes, caused by shifts in the Earth's crust, are far more common. Quakes occur daily, but most are minor tremors too small to be noticed. Every now and then, there is a major quake. Out at sea an earthquake can cause a *tsunami*, or tidal wave. When these giant walls of water reach land, they damage ports and flood coastal areas.

The city of Kōbe lies close to the center of an earthquake zone. On January 17, 1995, a major earthquake devastated the city. Some 6,000 people died, and buildings (like the one shown in the photo here) collapsed.

Nowadays Japan spends billions of yen each year on earthquake research in an effort to predict major quakes before they happen. That way, cities can be evacuated and many lives saved. In Japanese cities, buildings are designed

The Shifting Earth

The origins of the islands of Japan lie in movements of the Earth's vast tectonic plates—the rigid pieces that make up the Earth's outer shell. Like California, Japan lies in a region where two of these great plates meet and grind against one another. Over millions of years, the island chain of Japan formed where the Asian plate met and slowly collided with the Pacific plate. Enormous pressure caused the edges of the plates to buckle, on Kyūshū, regularly belches smoke and rains ash down on the surrounding region. People living in towns near the volcano are used to washing ash from their automobiles almost every week. In 1986, Mount Mihara, on Ō-shima Island, near Tokyo, erupted. Thousands of people living nearby had to be evacuated.

The Coastal Plains

Since the mountains are too steep for building and farming, most people live on the flat plains along the coasts or in narrow valleys. The fertile soil of the plains is made of fragments from the mountains, carried down by fast-flowing streams and rivers, and of sediment from the sea.

Only 15 percent of Japan is low-lying, yet 80 percent of the population live in the lowlands. Cities, factories, and farmlands are all crowded into coastal strips. Space is so tight that land has to be reclaimed from the sea. The largest lowland area is the Kantō Plain, on Honshū, where Tokyo stands.

Japanese Place-names

On a map of Japan, you will often find that place-names are followed by a hyphen plus a suffix (a word ending). The suffix indicates what kind of place it is. For example, the name Tanega-shima means Tanega-island.

A few other suffixes you will come across in this book are: *-wan* (bay), *-san* (mountain), *-hanto* (peninsula), *-ko* (lake), and *-ji* (Buddhist temple). In this book the full Japanese name is followed by a translation of the kind of place—for example, Tanega-shima Island.

Rivers and Lakes

Japan's rivers are short and fast-flowing. The longest river in Japan, the Shinano, flows just 228 miles (367 km) from the mountains of central Honshū down to the Sea of Japan. Japan's largest freshwater lake, Biwa-ko, is also in Honshū, northeast of Kyoto, and covers some 259 square miles (672 sq. km).

Japan's rivers and lakes have difficulty meeting the population's growing demand for freshwater. Japan has few natural reservoirs, and engineers find it difficult to build large dams in the rugged inland mountains.

REGIONS AND PREFECTURES OF JAPAN

Japan is divided into nine regions, called *chihō*, and further divided into 47 smaller divisions. Of these smaller areas, 43 are *ken,* known as prefectures in English. The remaining four are Tokyo, which has the status of *to,* or capital; Ōsaka and Kyōto, which are *fu,* or urban prefectures; and Hokkaidō, which is a *dō,* or district.

Listed below are the names of the prefectures and other divisions together with their capital (marked on the map with a dot). In Japanese the names of the *ken* are written Fukui-ken, Aichi-ken, and so on.

KEN (PREFECTURES)

1 AOMORI   Aomori
2 AKITA   Akita
3 IWATE   Morioka
4 MIYAGI   Sendai
5 YAMAGATA   Yamagata
6 FUKUSHIMA   Fukishima
7 IBARAKI   Mito
8 TOCHIGI   Utsunomiya
9 GUMMA   Maebashi
10 SAITAMA   Urawa
11 CHIBA   Chiba
12 KANAGAWA   Yokohama
13 NIIGATA   Niigata
14 YAMANASHI   Kōfu
15 SHIZUOKA   Shizuoka
16 NAGANO   Nagano
17 TOYAMA   Toyama
18 ISHIKAWA   Kanazawa
19 FUKUI   Fukui
20 GIFU   Gifu
21 AICHI   Nagoya
22 MIE   Tsu
23 SHIGA   Ōtsu
24 NARA   Nara
25 WAKAYAMA   Wakayama
26 HYŌGO   Kōbe
27 KAGAWA   Takamatsu
28 TOKUSHIMA   Tokushima
29 KŌCHI   Kōchi
30 EHIME   Matsuyama
31 TOTTORI   Tottori
32 OKAYAMA   Okayama

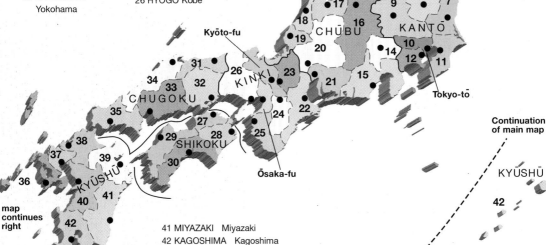

41 MIYAZAKI   Miyazaki
42 KAGOSHIMA   Kagoshima
43 OKINAWA   Naha

33 HIROSHIMA   Hiroshima
34 SHIMANE   Matsue
35 YAMAGUCHI   Yamaguchi
36 NAGASAKI   Nagasaki
37 SAGA   Saga
38 FUKUOKA   Fukuoka
39 ŌITA   Ōita
40 KUMAMOTO   Kumamoto

DŌ (DISTRICTS)
HOKKAIDŌ   Sapporo

FU (URBAN PREFECTURES)
29 ŌSAKA-FU   Ōsaka
26 KYŌTO-FU   Kyōto

TŌ (CAPITAL)
TOKYO-TŌ   Tokyo

THE REGIONS OF JAPAN

Throughout Japan's history, its rulers have divided the country in many different ways. Usually the country's political boundaries have been determined by its geography—by sea and by mountain. For example, a thousand years ago, the island of Honshū was divided into two. The lowlands west of the mountains that run down its middle were Kansai and those to the east, Kanto.

Today Japan is divided into nine regions. Each of the four main islands forms its own region, except the largest, Honshū, which is divided into five. The island of Okinawa and the surrounding islands form another region. Each of the regions has its own special character.

Hokkaidō: A Land of Snows

Hokkaidō is the most northerly of Japan's main islands. On the same latitude as Toronto, Hokkaidō has a colder climate than the rest of Japan. During the long, harsh winters, snow may cover the ground for up to four months. With an area of 30,077 square miles (77,900 sq. km), it is Japan's second-largest island, but it contains only 5 percent of Japan's population. Until 1900, Hokkaidō was regarded as a very remote region, and very few people lived there. Only the Ainu (*see* p. 50), some of the earliest inhabitants of Japan, were at home there.

The island is shaped like a diamond, with a hilly peninsula curving down toward Honshū. Off the northeast coast, the Kuril Islands are part of Russia, but Japan also claims them (*see* p. 69). Hokkaidō's economy is based on dairy farming, fishing, forestry, and tourism. The dairy-produce industry flourishes here because there is lots of land suitable for grazing cows.

This is the kanji *for* ken *("prefecture").*

This farm lies high up in the mountains of Hokkaidō. The steep-sided roofs help let the heavy snows that occur in the region slide off.

The most
northerly point
in Japan is the
Sōya Misaki
Cape, a few miles
from the port
of Wakkanai
and just a few
more from the
Russian island
of Sakhalin.

Central Hokkaidō is mountainous and mainly undeveloped. Bear and deer roam forested mountain slopes, and sheep and cattle graze high moorland pastures. Daisetsuzan National Park (*see* p. 32) is the largest wilderness area in Japan. The park is popular with tourists who want to hike or ski or just to enjoy the rugged scenery.

Hokkaidō's largest lowland area is the Ishikari Plain in the southwest. The city of Sapporo on the plain is Hokkaidō's capital and Japan's fifth-largest city. Unlike many other Japanese cities, Sapporo was carefully planned on a grid system with wide avenues, built with help from American advisors sent at the request of the governor of Hokkaidō in 1870. It is a popular ski resort and hosted the Winter Olympic Games in 1972. Every February people flock to the Sapporo Snow Festival. There they can enjoy winter sports or marvel at fantastic statues of animals and buildings carved from ice.

At the southwest tip of the island, the Seikan Tunnel crosses the Tsugaru-kaikyo Strait, running below the sea for over 33 miles (53 km). It links Hokkaidō with the mainland and is the world's second-longest tunnel, after the Channel Tunnel, which links France and Great Britain.

Honshū: Japan's Mainland

Honshū is Japan's largest island, and the Japanese think of it as the "mainland." Shaped like a boomerang, it curves to the southwest toward Korea. Nowhere on Honshū is more than 75 miles (120 km) from the sea. With an area of 89,124 square miles (230,831 sq. km), the island is roughly the size of Minnesota and is home to some 80 percent of the Japanese people.

Northern Honshū is the least-developed part of the island and has the harshest climate. Jagged mountain ranges run down the middle, with narrow coastal plains on either side. In central Honshū three mountain ranges known as the Japanese Alps form the highest mountains in Japan. East of these mountains is a chain of volcanoes, which includes Mount Fuji (*see* box opposite).

These are the kanji for Mount Fuji—Japan's holy mountain—which is located on Honshū.

Mount Fuji: Japan's Holy Mountain

The perfect, snow-capped cone of the volcano Mount Fuji is one of Japan's most powerful symbols (*see* p. 6). Serene and snow-covered for most of the year, its beauty has been a subject of Japanese art for hundreds of years. The wood-block print above, for example, is part of a series of pictures of the mountain by the famous Japanese artist Katsushika Hokusai (*see* p. 94). On a clear winter's day, Mount Fuji can be seen from Tokyo 60 miles (100 km) to the northeast.

There are different ideas about what the mountain's name means. Some say it means "everlasting"; others say the name comes from the Ainu language and means "fire." Japanese people revere the mountain greatly. Some believe that the mountain has a soul. Every July and August, thousands of pilgrims climb the mountain to visit its many temples or to watch the sun rise over the summit.

Mount Fuji in fact consists of three volcanoes, although lava from one—Shin Fuji, or "New Fuji"—has covered the other two and they can no longer be seen. Mount Fuji is dormant (inactive). It last erupted in 1707, scattering ash as far away as Tokyo.

In the north of Honshū is the Tohoku region. This remote and mountainous region has changed less quickly than many other parts of Japan. It was only in the 17th century that the area came under central government control. Life in its mountain villages, country towns, and hot-spring resorts is very traditional. There are few large industrial areas or major ports, and people often leave the region to find work. Those who remain make a living from farming—growing rice or raising cattle—or forestry.

The largest city, Sendai, has a population of more than 900,000. It is a modern city with broad boulevards and an efficient subway system. Sendai is full of students, who attend the city's eight universities.

The lowlands of the central Kantō and Chūbu regions are the most developed part of Honshū. In the east the large Kantō Plain slopes down to Tokyo Bay. It is the site of a vast urban area where Japan's capital, Tokyo (*see* pp. 33–39), merges into the cities of Kawasaki and Yokohama. Away from Tokyo are ancient religious sites such as Nikkō and Kamakura. Nikkō lies 85 miles (137 km) north of the capital. It is a collection of important religious shrines and temples, set against a backdrop of giant cedars more than 400 years old. The roofs and walls of the buildings are decorated with intricate carvings of animals and birds.

The coastal strip south from Tokyo to Yokohama is the most densely populated part of Japan. The cities here look much like American cities, with towering skyscrapers and broad highways. Beyond Mount Fuji and into Shizuoka prefecture, rows of neat green bushes ring the hillsides, forming the large plantations that produce Japan's finest teas. The next major city is Nagoya, an important industrial center. At the nearby city of Toyota, automobiles are manufactured; other factories produce chemicals and textile machines.

In the center of Honshū are the Japanese Alps where people visit ski resorts in winter. After a day spent skiing, they often go to nearby hot-spring resorts (*see* box opposite) and relax in a hot tub. In summer the mountains around Matsumoto attract hikers and climbers.

In Kōbe a cablecar takes visitors up Mount Rokko, where there is a spectacular view over the city's harbor.

Natural Hot Tubs

Japan's volcanic terrain has one big advantage: the hot springs, or *onsen*, that bubble up from deep within the Earth where water is heated by molten rock. Resorts have grown up around the springs, and visitors come to bathe and relax in the steaming waters.

According to legend, the first baths were founded at Dogo Onsen, near Matsuyama, almost 3,000 years ago. Over the centuries, many famous people came to relax at the resort, including some of the earliest emperors, great Buddhist teachers, poets, and novelists. The present bathhouse was built in the Meiji period (1868–1912). It has a spectacular roof that rises in several tiers with upward-curving eaves. As visitors walk the short distance from their hotels to the hots springs, the *geta* (Japanese clogs) they wear make a clattering sound on the cobblestoned streets.

Inside the bathhouse visitors change into a *yukata*, something like a light cotton *kimono*, then make their way into the ancient stone baths. Sitting on wooden stools, they wash carefully, rinse off the soap, then get into the bath and relax in the bubbling hot water. The *onsen* water is known to relieve physical ailments such as rheumatism and arthritis, but most people visit the baths to relax their bodies and unwind from the stresses of work. The resort of Beppu, Kyūshū, shown above, is one of Japan's most popular *onsen* resorts.

At high tide the sea floods the gateway, or torii, to the Itsukushima shrine, on Mija-jima Island, southern Honshū. In early times the island was sacred and people could not walk on it. To visit the temple, they had to approach the shrine from the sea, entering through the "floating" gateway.

On Honshū's northwestern coast are two historical cities—Kanazawa and Toyama. Kanazawa's old winding streets and alleys are lined by traditional homes and shops. It is a well-known center for arts, where local people perform in traditional *nō* theater (*see* p. 97) and comedy plays. Toyama has also been an important center for oriental medicine since the 17th century.

To the southwest, in Kinki region, the cities of Ōsaka and Kōbe stand on the Ōsaka Plain. Together with Kyōto they form a triangular industrial area, second in importance only to the Tokyo–Yokohama area. Ōsaka is Japan's third-largest city and home to Japan's puppet theater, called *bunraku* (*see* pp. 97–98). The ancient capitals, Kyōto (*see* pp. 42–43) and Nara, lie close by. Lake Biwa-ko, Japan's largest lake, is only a short distance from Kyōto. It is named after the musical instrument called a *biwa* because the shape of the lake is similar.

Southwestern Honshū—Chūgoku—is divided into two parts by the Chūgoku Mountains, which run from east to west. The coast of San-in, the northern part, is battered by the Sea of Japan. San-yo, the area south of the mountains, is on the Inland Sea and has a milder climate. Cities and farmlands are set in small pockets of lowland.

The city of Hiroshima (*see* pp. 44–45), toward the southern end of Honshū, stands on a large bay. In the bay the beautiful island of Miya-jima has a very famous shrine. A graceful red gateway, or *torii*, to the shrine stands in the sea. At the southern tip of Honshū is Shimonoseki, a seaport and industrial city, which is linked by a tunnel to Kitakyūshū in Kyūshū.

Shikoku

Shikoku, Japan's smallest main island, lies off the south coast of western Honshū, across the Inland Sea. With an area of 7,258 square miles (18,798 sq. km), the island is smaller than New Jersey and is home to just 3 percent of Japan's population. Until recent times Shikoku was known as a quiet backwater. Today, however, three major bridge networks connect Shikoku with Honshū (*see* pp. 88–89).

Although it has a mild climate, Shikoku is relatively undeveloped. Mountain ranges run from west to east across the island, making inland areas hard to reach. There are no major lowland areas, and towns, industrial centers, and farmlands are all crowded into narrow coastal strips. The largest cities—Matsuyama, Takamatsu, and Tokushima—are on the northern coast. Rice, wheat, oranges, and tobacco are grown along the coast on land not occupied by factories or towns.

Shikoku is a popular pilgrimage center. On the island are 88 temples built in honor of Kūkai, a Buddhist monk who was born on Shikoku in 774. Kūkai helped introduce the Buddhist religion to Japan and was honored as a Buddhist saint. Spring is the favorite season for making the pilgrimage. Pilgrims dress in a white kimono, leggings, and mittens. Some make the pilgrimage on foot, taking two months to walk round the 88 temples, while others go by bus and finish in two weeks.

On the east coast of Shikoku is a spectacular natural feature—the Naruto Whirlpools. These form in the narrow channel that separates Shikoku from Awaji-shima Island. A difference in the sea level on each side of the channel pulls the tides into a whirling mass of water that breaks on the rocks along the coast.

The Seto–Chuo Expressway connecting northern Shikoku with Honshū was opened in 1988. In fact it is a series of six bridges and four viaducts that hop from island to island across the Inland Sea. Altogether the bridges span some 7.5 miles (12 km).

The longest single-span suspension bridge in the world is in Japan. The Akashi Kaikyō Bridge connects southeast Honshū with Awaji-shima Island.

Kyūshū: "Silicon Island"

Kyūshū is Japan's most southern main island. With an area of 17,135 square miles (44,380 sq. km), it is the third-largest island in Japan and is home to 11 percent of the population. After Honshū it is the most developed island. Kyūshū has the nickname "Silicon Island" because of its vibrant computer and microchip industry.

Four mountain ranges run north to south across the island. The enormous Mount Aso volcano caldera (crater) lies in the northeast, at the heart of a beautiful national park. The mountain has five summits and the largest caldera in the world. The central peak, Mount Nakadake, is an active volcano that regularly billows smoke. East of the national park, the port of Beppu is famous for its hot springs (*see* p. 23).

Most of Kyūshū's population lives on the narrow strips of lowland between the sea and the inland mountains. Here wheatfields lie in a checkerboard pattern on the land along the shore of Isahaya Bay.

Kyūshū enjoys a semitropical climate, with long, hot summers and mild winters. Its jagged western shore is dotted with islands. The port of Nagasaki lies on the west coast. From the 17th century to the mid-19th, when the rest of Japan was closed to foreigners, Nagasaki was visited by Dutch traders. Gradually Nagasaki became an important center for trade and Western learning. In

1945 the city was the target of the second atomic bomb dropped by the United States.

Most of Kyūshū's population live on small patches of lowland in the north and west. The largest cities, Fukuoka and Kitakyūshū, lie on the north coast. At the Kanmon Strait, near Kitakyūshū, only a mile (1.6 km) of water separates Kyūshū from Honshū. Road and rail tunnels under the strait carry traffic between the two islands.

The Ryūkū Kingdom

Until the 1870s, the Ryūkū Islands were an independent kingdom. In the 15th century, the Ryūkū kings united all the islands for the first time and ruled the kingdom from Shuri Castle in Okinawa's present-day capital, Naha. The Ryūkū people were peaceful traders, and they had their own colorful culture, influenced by nearby Chinese Taiwan.

In 1609, however, a Japanese clan from southern Kyūshū invaded the islands and the Ryūkū kings became its vassals. In the late 19th century, Japan formally annexed Okinawa and set up military bases on the islands.

Smaller Islands

The Ryūkyū and the Bonins are two groups of islands that lie south of the main islands of Japan. The Ryūkyū Islands are a chain of some 100 craggy islands that stretch some 700 miles (1,130 km) from Kyūshū, almost to Taiwan. They have a subtropical climate with lush vegetation. Altogether the Ryūkyū are home to about a million people. Tourists flock there to enjoy the sandy beaches and to dive or snorkel in the clear, blue waters around the islands' coral reefs.

Okinawa in the southern Ryūkyū is the largest island, with an area of 450 square miles (1,166 sq. km), and is a region in its own right. In the 19th century, the martial art of karate originated on Okinawa. After World War II, the Ryūkyū Islands were occupied by the United States. The northern group was returned to Japan in 1953, and the southern group in 1972. There are still a number of American military bases on the islands.

The Bonin Islands, a group of 97 islands, lie 600 miles (970 km) southeast of Japan. After World War II, they were occupied by U.S. forces but were returned in 1968. Crops of sugarcane, bananas, and pineapples are grown.

The most southern islands of Okinawa prefecture—and of Japan—are the Yaeyama Islands, which lie just north of the Tropic of Cancer.

JAPAN'S CLIMATE

The Japanese are fascinated by their country's weather. After greeting one another, people almost always talk about the weather and the changing seasons.

The enormous north–south range of Japan's territory means that the country encompasses very different climates. In the far north, Hokkaidō's climate is like Siberia's, with short, cool summers and long, cold, and snowy winters. Temperatures in winter may fall as low as 14°F (-10°C); while on a warm summer day, the temperature may rise to 73°F (23°C).

In Okinawa, in the Ryūkyū Islands in the far south, the climate is subtropical, with hot summers and warm winters. Summers are scorching, with temperatures as high as 90°F (32°C), while winter temperatures rarely fall below 50°F (10°C). Temperatures also fall with altitude, so the peaks of high mountains are often many degrees cooler than the lowlands below.

Japan's position between the Pacific Ocean and the Asian landmass, together with the great north–south length of the archipelago, create a very complex climate. Sapporo, on the west coast of Hokkaidō, has long, snow-filled winters. Tokyo, by contrast, has very cold winters but hardly any snow.

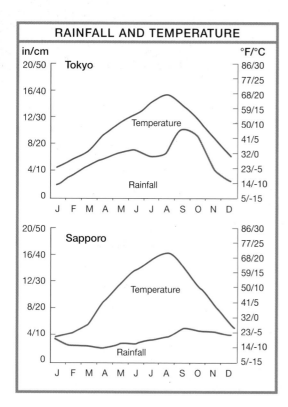

Monsoons and Currents

Monsoons are seasonal winds that bring different weather to western and eastern parts of Japan. In winter, cold winds blowing from northwest Asia bring cool air to northern Japan and cause rain and snow to fall on western coasts. In summer, moist winds from the Pacific make southern and central areas hot and humid.

Ocean currents also affect Japan's climate. The Japan Current is a warm sea current that flows east along southern coasts as far as Tokyo Bay, warming the land. Another warm current, the Kuroshio Current, flows along western shores. In winter it warms the air, but it also increases rainfall. Farther north the cold Oyashio Current flows down from the Arctic to cool the eastern shore of Hokkaidō. Where it meets warmer waters flowing from the south, fogs often form.

The Seasons

Because Japan is situated in the Northern Hemisphere, its seasons fall at roughly the same time as they do in the United States and Europe. December through February are the coldest months. The arrival of spring is marked by the blossoming of cherry trees. All over Japan people celebrate the cherry blossoms with a festival called *hanami*, meaning "flower viewing." Families gather to picnic on mats spread beneath the flowering branches.

Women in traditional dress shelter under umbrellas as they leave a Shinto shrine. Japan gets plenty of rainfall. Almost everywhere in Japan, there are more than 40 inches (100 cm) of rain each year, with most rain falling in late spring and fall.

Cherry blossom time is followed by a rainy season that lasts about two months. Summers are hot and humid, with temperatures highest in August. Many Japanese leave the scorching cities at this time and head for the cool of the mountains.

Fall is the season of typhoons. These tropical storms sweep in from the Pacific, bringing torrential rains and rough seas to the southeast. As many as 30 typhoons may hit Japan each year, uprooting trees and wrecking ships and houses. The strong winds of up to 125 miles per hour (200 km/h) mostly blow themselves out before they reach the Tokyo Plain.

The stormy season is followed by a period of mild, clear weather in October and early November. Many tourists choose to visit Japan at this time, as fall turns the trees to a blaze of color, and before the winter chill sets in. This is another time when the Japanese like to admire the colors of nature.

WILDLIFE AND PLANTS

The great north–south distance in Japan means that a huge variety of plants and animals live there, including both tropical and Arctic species. Some 17,000 plant species are found among Japan's rich vegetation.

A Land of Trees and Flowers

Forests cover 68 percent of the land in Japan. On hills and mountains, many native plants survive, but in the lowlands, natural vegetation has been replaced by farms and cities. Different trees exist in various regions. In southern Japan, palm and camphor trees and tree ferns flourish. Bamboo groves sprout in river valleys, and subtropical coasts are ringed with mangrove swamps.

In temperate central Honshū, red cedar trees are prized for timber. Broadleaved species include oak, chestnut, beech, and maple. Farther north, broadleaved forests give way to evergreens. On Hokkaidō, conifer (cone-bearing) trees dominate, including spruce, larch, and fir.

All over Japan, the seasonal flowering of well-loved plants is greeted with festivals and celebrations. Cherry and other fruit trees blossom in spring. Lotus flowers appear in August, and the chrysanthemum, both the imperial and national flower, in November.

The sika is a species of deer found in the forests of east Asia. The Japanese sika is the smallest kind, just 30–34 inches (80–86 cm) to the shoulder. In winter the sika's coat is gray brown, but in summer it is reddish with brown spots.

Mammals and Birds

Japan's animals are less varied than its plants, but the islands are still home to 140 different mammals, 450 birds, and many reptiles and insects. Common mammals include foxes, badgers, squirrels, mice, and bats. Graceful sika deer have reddish coats spotted with brown in summer and darker fur in winter. The

red-faced monkey, or Japanese macaque, is also common. In northern Honshū, troops of macaques keep warm in winter by bathing in hot springs.

Japan's birds include many waterbirds, including cranes, herons, swans, ducks, and cormorants. Land birds include sparrows, swallows, thrushes, nightingales, and robins. The giant salamander of Japan is the largest amphibian in the world.

The steamy south and snowy north have their own animal species. The Ryūkyū Islands, south of Kyūhū, are home to the Ryūkyū rabbit and the rare spiny mouse. Tropical fish and deadly seasnakes swim in the warm waters among the coral reefs. In the north of Japan, Hokkaidō is home to red deer, brown bear, and subarctic birds such as the raven and eagle owl.

The Environment

Japan does not have a good reputation in environmental matters and is a regular target for environmental groups such as Greenpeace. Japan, along with Iceland and Norway, is one of the world's three countries that permit whaling. Dolphins regularly fall prey to the widespread Japanese practice of driftnet fishing, and every year some 30,000 hawksbill turtles, an endangered species, are slaughtered for their valuable shells.

Japanese macaques, sometimes known as snow monkeys, have thick rugged fur to protect them from the icy cold of Honshū. The macaques also like to keep warm by bathing in the region's hot

Driftnet fishing involves two boats, which may be anything up to 30 miles (50 km) apart, hauling a fine net between them and catching everything—from tuna to dolphin—in their path.

31

JAPAN'S NATIONAL PARKS

Japan's national parks are found throughout the country, from the northern tips of Hokkaidō (Shiretoko and Rishiri-Rebun-Sarobetsu national parks) to the most southerly islands (Iriomote-jima Island). They include unspoiled coastlines (Kirishima-Yaku), volcanoes (Kirishima), lakes and forests (Akan), lonely islands (Inland Sea), and swampland (Kushiro Shitsugen). The largest of the parks is the Daisetsuzan National Park in Hokkaidō, which covers some 890 square miles (2,310 sq. km) of forest, lakes, and volcanoes.

Rishiri-Rebun-Sarobetsu

Shiretoko

HOKKAIDŌ

Akan

Daisetsuzan

Shikotsu-Tōya

Kushiro Shitsugen

Towada-Hachimantai

Rikuchu Kaigan

Bandai-Asahi

Nikkō

HONSHŪ

Chūbu Sangaku

Hakusan

Jōshin-Etsu-Kōgen

Inland Sea

Chichibu-Tama

Aso-Kujuu

Minami-Alps

Ise-Shima

Saikai

Yoshino-Kumano

Fuji-Hakone-Izu

Unzen Amakusa

KYŪSHŪ

SHIKOKU

Kirishima

Kyūshū-Chūōsanchi

Kirishima-Yaku

Iriomote-jima Island

Japan is also the world's biggest consumer of tropical rain-forest timber. A great deal of the wood goes to produce disposable chopsticks, or *waribashi*, for Japan's restaurants and noodle bars. Japan's own forests, too, are falling prey to pollution, acid rain, and the spread of towns and cities.

The cramped conditions on Japanese islands means that many species that were once common are now at risk of dying out altogether. The crested ibis, once a familiar sight, is now close to extinction, as is the Japanese crane. Brown bears once roamed forests throughout Japan. This powerful bear can grow to a height of more than 6 feet (2 m). Now they have been hunted to extinction, except on Hokkaidō, where only a few hundred bears remain.

Despite this neglect of the environment, Japan does have a large number of national parks. These were set up to help preserve the wild areas of Japan, particularly in the far north and the far south of the country.

THE CITIES

Japan's population lives overwhelmingly in towns and cities. Sometimes the cities are so close to one another that they merge, creating vast urban sprawls. Japan's big cities are vibrant places, full of energy and color. New, exciting buildings are always appearing on their skylines, and modern transportation networks hurtle their busy inhabitants from place to place.

Tokyo—Japan's Capital

Tokyo is the capital of Japan and the seat of its government. It is also the main center of business, broadcasting, art, and fashion in Japan. The city stands in the heart of the Kanto Plain, facing Tokyo Bay on the Pacific coast. More than eight million people live within the city limits, but its suburbs sprawl over the plain to merge with the port of Yokohama and other towns. Altogether Greater Tokyo has a population of 25 million people and is one of the largest cities in the world.

　　The capital began life as a tiny fishing village called Edo (meaning "gate of the inlet"), on the banks of the Sumida-gawa River. Edo lay at a junction of important trading routes, and in the 1400s, a lord built a castle here to guard this important point. In 1590,

東京

The Japanese write the name of their capital with two kanji. The first kanji (tō) means "east" while the second (kyō) means "capital." Tokyo lies on Japan's east coast.

This woodcut shows 19th-century Edo— later Tokyo—a busy city of wooden houses and broad streets.

DOWNTOWN TOKYO

The city of Tokyo is divided into 23 wards, called *ku* in Japanese. Within the wards are many smaller, traditional areas such as Ginza and Ueno.

Through the crowded, bustling cityscape of office buildings, museums, department stores, and temples, and across rivers, canals, and docks, runs the overhead road network known as the Shuto Expressway. Today the expressway's 30 sections exceed 136 miles (220 km) in length and in parts is as high as 130 feet (40 m). The expressway carries some 1,130,000 automobiles a day.

SHIBUYA-KU

SHIBUYA

EBISU

HIRŌ

SHUTO EXPRESSWAY

Meiji-jingū Inner Garden

HARAJUKU

AOYAMA

Aoyama Cemetery

Meiji-jingū Outer Garden

Tenru-ji Temple

Shinjuku-Gyoen Garden

SHINJUKU-KU

SHUTO EXPRESSWAY

National Nō Theater

Meiji-jingū Theater

National Diet Building

National Theater

MINATO-KU

Imperial Palace

Imperial Gardens

CHIYODA-KU

National Museum of Modern Art

Science Museum

BUNKYO-KU

SHUTO

Kanda-gawa River

SHUTO EXPRESS WAY

Idemitsu Museum of Art

GINZA

Tokyo Station

SHUTO EXPRESSWAY

UENO

Ueno Zoo

Ueno Park

TAITŌ-KU

ASAKUSA

Tokyo National Museum

National Science Museum

National Museum of Western Art

Sensō-ji Temple

N

SHUTO

EXPRESSWAY

Tsukiji market

TOKYO PORT

Tokyo Stock Exchange

Sumida-gawa

SHUTO EXPRESSWAY

CHŪŌ-KU

SUMIDA-KU

Sumo stadium

Edo-Tokyo Museum

TOKYO SUBWAY

Map labels:
Ikebukuro · Sungamo · Oji · Kita-Senju · Ayase · Nishi-Nippori · Nerima · Ogikubo · Nakano · Korakuen · Suidōbashi · Asakusa · Asakusabashi · Motoyawata · Nishi-Funabashi · Nakano-Sakaue · Shinjuku · Iidabashi · Ueno · Ichigaya · Ogawa-Machi · Akihabara · Yotsuya · Kudanashita · Kanda · Shinjukusanchōme · Nagatacho · Otemachi · Higashi Nihombashi · Aoyamaitchōme · Kokkagijidō-mae · Mitsuko-shimae · Akasakmitsuke · Tōkyo · Nihombashi · Ningyocho · Shibuya · Yarakucho · Hibiya · Omotesando · Tameike-sannō · Kasumigaseki · Kayabacho · Ebisu · Ginza · Hatchōbori · Gotanda · Mita · Higashi-Ginza · Shin-Kiba · Shimbashi · Shinagawa

Legend:
- Ginza
- Marunouchi
- Hibiya
- Tozai
- Chiyoda
- Yurakucho
- Teio
- Hanzomon
- Toei Asakusa
- Toei Mita
- Namboku
- Toei Shinjuku
- - - East Japan Railway
- Junction

Tokyo's subway system may look complicated, but in fact it is the simplest way of getting around the city.

a powerful warlord named Tokugawa Ieyasu took over the castle and rebuilt it. When he became shogun, or supreme general of Japan, in 1603, Edo became the center of the nation's government. During the 17th century, the Tokugawa family continued to rule Japan from Edo.

By the 18th century, Edo was home to a million people and was probably the largest city in the world. Apart from their roofs, the houses and even important buildings were made out of wood, making them vulnerable to devastating fires.

In the 19th century, the power of the shoguns passed back to the emperor. In 1868, Emperor Meiji moved his capital from the city of Kyōto to Tokyo. The castle became the emperor's palace. Tokyo's full official name became Tokyo-to, meaning "east capital prefecture" because the city lay on Japan's east coast. This name is used for administrative purposes and for postal addresses. Usually, however, the name is shortened to Tokyo.

Throughout its history, Tokyo has been ravaged by war and disaster many times. In 1657, fires gutted nearly

Visiting businessmen and commuters who are too late to catch the last train home often stay overnight in a capsule hotel. Each capsule measures about 7 feet by 3 feet by 3 feet (2 x 1 x 1 m) and contains a bed, TV, radio, and alarm clock.

half the city. Nearly three centuries later, in 1923, much of the capital was destroyed in the Great Kanto Earthquake (*see* p. 62). During World War II (1941–1945), Allied bombing flattened Tokyo. Both times new buildings rose from the ruins. The result is a mainly modern city, with only a few old buildings. Overhead expressways tower over ancient narrow streets, and shiny skyscrapers dwarf tiny, more traditional houses and shops.

In Tokyo, as in most of Japan's lowland areas, space is cramped. There are few parks in the city center. In Tokyo Bay whole new districts have been reclaimed from the sea for factories and gardens. Every weekday tens of thousands of office workers surge into Tokyo's downtown. During rush hour the streets are jammed with automobiles. Subways are so packed that officials called "pushers" are employed to cram as many people as possible on each train.

Housing is also cramped and very expensive. Visiting businessmen sometimes sleep in "capsule hotels," where each tiny room is the size of a large locker, with space only for a bed, and perhaps a TV and telephone.

There is much to see in Tokyo, but foreigners often find it difficult to get around. Few streets have names,

A Fast-changing City

Throughout its history, Tokyo has been rebuilt many times—whether because of earthquake, fire, or war. Even today—when Japan is peaceful and buildings are built to be earthquake-proof—the cityscape is constantly changing. One of Japan's most famous architects, Toyo Ito, has written: "Today in Tokyo buildings are constructed and demolished at a bewildering speed. It is really stunning.

Buildings invade the city and gain popularity, then, just as quickly, they are used up and discarded like a piece of paper." In the 1980s and early 1990s, Japan was so rich that business corporations could afford to put up buildings almost as if they were pasting up an advertisement.

The new buildings display an astonishing variety of styles. In the

busy shopping area of Shibuya—there is the rocketlike Humax Pavilion, where young people come to shop, and meet friends. In Shibuya, too, is the beautiful new National Nō Theater, where performances of Japan's ancient theater take place in a stately atmosphere. Overlooking the Sumida-gawa River is the apartment house pictured here, curving like a white flame. The most spectacular structure in Tokyo, though, isn't a building at all, but the vast network of overhead roads that fly over the busy cityscape—the Shuto Expressway (*see* p. 34).

Like New York City, Tokyo is a fast-paced, nonstop city. In busy Ginza ward, shoppers throng the street beneath hundreds of store signs (see also p. 87).

and houses are not numbered systematically. If tourists do get lost, there are special yellow tourist phones that will help them on their way.

The capital is divided into 23 *ku*, or wards. Each of these districts is like a little town, with its own identity. The heart of the city is Chiyoda ward, where the Imperial Palace (*see* p. 12) lies close to the Central Station. The Imperial Palace is home to the emperor and empress of Japan and his family. The palace stands in its own gardens, surrounded by high walls and a moat. The east palace garden is always open to the public, but the inner gardens can only be visited twice a year, on the emperor's birthday (December 23) and during the New Year's holiday on January 2.

South of Central Station lies Ginza, Tokyo's famous shopping area. In the late 19th century, its department stores were among the first brick buildings in Japan. South of Ginza is the Tsukiji Fish Market (*see* p. 80), where in the early morning the fish stalls gleam with squid, crabs, and other seafoods loved by the Japanese.

Ueno is best known for its beautiful park; it can take a whole day to explore its sights. In early April, the Japanese flock to the park to see the cherry blossoms. The park includes a lake, the oldest zoo in Japan, and many shrines and temples, including the Doll Temple. Museums in the park include the Tokyo National Museum, the Museum of Natural Science, and the Museum of Western Art.

Asakusa was once Tokyo's entertainment area, where people in a festive mood came to the *kabuki* theaters and teahouses. Today little remains of the old district, which was largely destroyed during World War II. The district's heart, Senso-ji Temple, was rebuilt. Inside is an ancient golden statue of the Buddhist goddess of mercy. According to legend, fishermen discovered the statue in the nearby Sumida-gawa River in A.D. 628.

Shibuya ward is popular with young people. They come to shop in the huge department stores, and often meet friends at the Shibuya Station beside the statue of Hachiko. Hachiko was a dog who each day waited outside the station for his master to come home from work. One day his master died at work, and Hachiko waited in vain. The dog continued to wait loyally for the next ten years until he, too, died.

In the late 19th century, Asakusa was the site of Japan's first movie theaters.

Kamakura

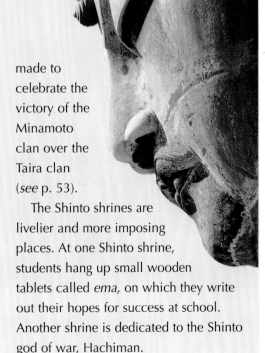

Visitors to Tokyo who want to escape the hectic pace of life in the city often go to the ancient city of Kamakura for calm. It was the capital of Japan between 1185 and 1333, when the Minamoto clan ruled Japan as shoguns. The city became an important religious center, and today there are more than 70 temples and shrines there.

The Zen Buddhist temples and their gardens are quiet places, ideal for the meditation that this kind of Buddhism advises (*see* p. 52). The most famous sight is a bronze statue of the Buddha 36 feet (11 m) high. The Great Buddha dates back to the 13th century and weighs almost 935 tons (850 t). According to legend the statue was made to celebrate the victory of the Minamoto clan over the Taira clan (*see* p. 53).

The Shinto shrines are livelier and more imposing places. At one Shinto shrine, students hang up small wooden tablets called *ema*, on which they write out their hopes for success at school. Another shrine is dedicated to the Shinto god of war, Hachiman.

These are the Japanese characters for Ōsaka.

Ōsaka: A City of Business

Ōsaka is Japan's third-largest city. For a long time, the city was the country's main trading center—ships from all over Japan and farther afield sailed into Ōsaka Bay and merchants thronged the city streets. Today Ōsaka is still a busy, thriving city. In 1996, the total revenue from Ōsaka's economic product was higher than the gross national products (GNPs) of all but the top eight economies in the world—higher, even, than those of Australia and Mexico.

The Ōsakans are very business minded and they work hard. They speak their own gritty, colorful dialect and have rough-and-ready manners that can shock the more refined inhabitants of Kyōto. People greeting each other in the streets often begin by asking "*Mō kari makka?*" meaning "Are you making any money?"

Ōsaka was heavily bombed during World War II. Today its skyline is dominated by concrete and glass sky-scrapers and elevated expressways. Seven subway lines and fleets of buses carry the busy Ōsakans around the city. Canals and rivers crisscross the city, and on hot summer days, visitors and Ōsakans take to boats that cruise the waterways. There are some spectacular mod-ern buildings. The spaceship-like Ōsaka Dome is home to the local baseball team, and down in the harbor, the Aquarium has the world's largest fishtank, inhabited by two whale sharks.

Visitors usually come to Ōsaka, however, to see its famous castle (*jō*). The original castle was built for the warlord Toyotomi Hideyoshi, who in the 16th century conquered all of Japan. Some 50,000 people labored for three years to build the stronghold. The streets around Ōsaka-jō Castle were built like a maze, so that an army approaching the castle could easily be ambushed or trapped by the castle's defenders.

After Hideyoshi's death, the head of the rival Tokugawa clan laid siege to the castle and left it in ruins. The castle was later rebuilt, but since then it has been repeatedly destroyed and rebuilt. Today there is only a concrete reproduction of the castle's eight-story tower.

Ōsakans are particularly proud of their city's tradition of *bunraku* puppet theater (*see* pp. 97–98). The city is home to the National Bunraku Theater, and the most famous *bunraku* playwright, Chikamatsu Monzaemon, wrote plays about the merchants and other inhabitants of the city.

Young people sometimes like to go to Panasonic Square, which has displays of the latest electronic gadgetry. There are lots of virtual-reality games to try out.

Osaka's downtown is divided between the business-dominated Kita ward in the north and the entertainment quarter of Minami.

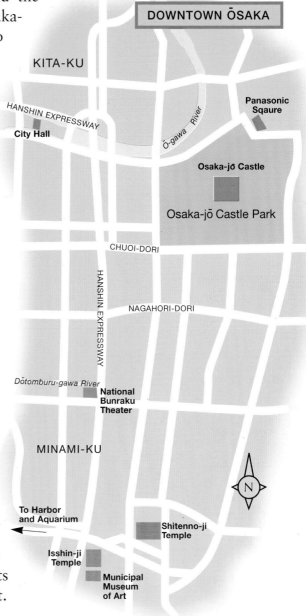

DOWNTOWN ŌSAKA

KITA-KU

HANSHIN EXPRESSWAY

City Hall

Ō-gawa River

Panasonic Sqaure

Osaka-jō Castle

Osaka-jō Castle Park

CHUOI-DORI

HANSHIN EXPRESSWAY

NAGAHORI-DORI

Dōtomburu-gawa River

National Bunraku Theater

MINAMI-KU

N

To Harbor and Aquarium

Shitenno-ji Temple

Isshin-ji Temple

Municipal Museum of Art

京都

The name Kyōto
is written with two
kanji—kyō and to—
both of which mean
"capital." Kyōto was
Japan's capital city for
more than 1,000 years.

Kyōto: The "Heart of Japan"

The ancient and beautiful city of Kyōto in central Honshū was home to the emperors of Japan for more than 1,000 years. To the Japanese, Kyōto is *Nihon no Furusato*, the "heart of Japan." The city has many historic buildings, including 250 Shinto shrines and 1,500 Buddhist temples, but there are also modern shops and restaurants, gardens, museums, and a zoo.

Kyōto was the capital of Japan from 794 to 1868. The city was built by the emperor Kammu (736–806). He laid out the network of streets following the example of the

DOWNTOWN KYŌTO

Central Kyōto is contained within a grid of streets. This map shows the major streets (*dōri*) and wards (*ku*) that make up the traditional heart of the city. This grid system makes it easy to navigate. Kyōto addresses are given as the name of the nearest intersection plus their location *agaru* (up) or *sagaru* (down) from the intersection.

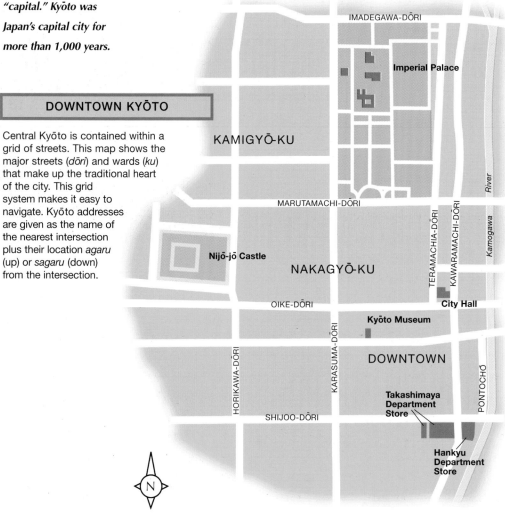

ancient capital of China, Chang'an (modern Xi'an). Throughout the centuries, Japan's most skillful artists flocked to the capital to work for the emperor, and the city blossomed as a center for arts and crafts. Over the years, parts of the city were destroyed by fire and earthquake and rebuilt. Unlike so many of Japan's historic cities, Kyōto was not bombed during World War II.

Kammu also built himself a palace, but the present imperial palace dates mostly from the 19th century. It includes the ceremonial hall where Japan's emperors were once crowned. The buildings are very simple and stand in expanses of dazzling white gravel and clipped green lawns.

The heart of today's city, however, is Nijō-jō Castle, built by the shogun Tokugawa Ieyasu at the beginning of the 17th century. The shoguns were warlords based in Tokyo (Edo) whose power challenged the supremacy of the emperors. Nijō-jō Castle has mighty fortifications, with thick walls and a moat. Inside there are "nightingale" floors. These were designed so that if anyone—an assassin or a thief—tried to move quietly down the corridors at night, the boards would squeak, or "sing like a nightingale."

On the outskirts of central Kyōto are many beautiful temples. The Golden Pavilion Temple stands three stories high, and each story has a roof covered with gold leaf. In the nearby Temple of the Peaceful Dragon is a garden with 15 rocks set into carefully raked, white gravel. The Chionin Temple houses the heaviest temple bell in Japan. It takes 17 monks to ring the bell. Close by, the Heian Shrine has painted red columns and roofs of glazed green tiles. The Temple of Clear Water to the south is built on a hillside. From its large wooden veranda, there are fine views of the city.

Kyoto's Nijō-jō Castle has a commanding view of the city. The castle belonged to the shoguns, who ruled from Tokyo. Its massive walls and watchtowers dwarfed the imperial palace—for hundreds of years the home of Japan's emperors.

43

*The kanji for Hiroshima
mean "broad island."*

Hiroshima: City of War and Peace

The prosperous city of Hiroshima lies on six sandy islands in the delta of the Ōta-gawa River, in southwestern Honshū. It was established in the 16th century when a local warlord built a moated castle on the site.

Today the city is famous less for its sights than for the terrible moment on August 6, 1945, when the U.S. Army Air Force dropped the world's first atomic bomb (*see* pp. 66–67). The blast flattened the city, killing in an instant some 75,000 people. The survivors suffered physical and mental scars, and many inhabitants of Hiroshima continue to suffer the consequences of the blast today.

The Children's Peace Memorial

In the Peace Memorial Park is the Children's Peace Memorial—a bronze statue of a young girl holding aloft a crane. In Japan the crane is a symbol of happiness and long life. After the war, many children fell sick with leukemia—a cancer of the blood that, in this instance, was caused by the radiation from the Hiroshima bomb blast. One girl, Sadako, developed leukemia at age ten. She became convinced that she would get better if she folded 1,000 paper cranes. She died having completed 644 cranes. The people of Hiroshima put up a statue in her honor and as a memorial to all the children who died because of the blast. Even today Japanese schoolchildren make paper cranes in memory of Sadako and send them in boxloads to decorate the monument.

The surviving inhabitants began to rebuild their city in 1950. Many of the streets and buildings of the present-day downtown are memorials to those who died in the blast. Every year thousands of visitors come to the city, which has become a powerful symbol for those who believe that nuclear weapons should be banned.

Not all of the city was rebuilt. Close to the spot where the bomb exploded are the ruins of the Industrial Promotion Hall. The building—now called the Atomic Bomb Memorial Dome—has been left as it was found after the blast. Across the river is the Peace Memorial Park, laid out in 1955 as a place to pray for peace. In the park is a saddle-shaped cenotaph. Beneath the cenotaph is a stone chest in which there is a scroll listing the names of all those who died in the blast. There is also a perpetual flame. When the last nuclear weapon on Earth has been destroyed, the flame will be put out. The park also holds the Children's Peace Memorial (*see* box opposite).

Nearby is the Peace Memorial Museum, which tells the harrowing story of the blast and its aftermath. Its exhibits include the burned "shadow" of a person who was incinerated by the intense heat and a model of the city after the blast.

The old castle has also been rebuilt and houses a museum of the city's history. Every year on August 6, the people of Hiroshima float paper lanterns down the Ōtagawa River in memory of those who died in the blast.

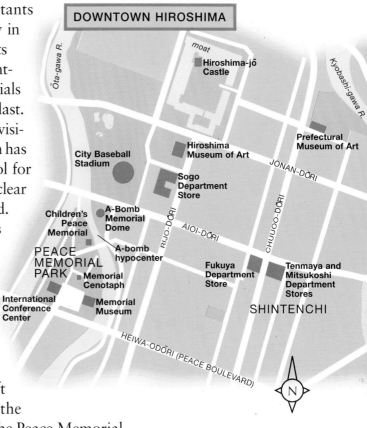

DOWNTOWN HIROSHIMA

Ōta-gawa R.
moat
Kyobashi-gawa R.
Hiroshima-jō Castle
City Baseball Stadium
Hiroshima Museum of Art
Prefectural Museum of Art
JONAN-DŌRI
Sogo Department Store
Children's Peace Memorial
A-Bomb Memorial Dome
A-bomb hypocenter
RIJO-DŌRI
AIOI-DŌRI
CHUUOO-DŌRI
PEACE MEMORIAL PARK
Memorial Cenotaph
Fukuya Department Store
Tenmaya and Mitsukoshi Department Stores
International Conference Center
Memorial Museum
SHINTENCHI
HEIWA-ODŌRI (PEACE BOULEVARD)
N

Central Hiroshima is built on islands in the Ōta-gawa River delta. The monuments to the people who died in the atomic-bomb blast of 1945 are all around the area of the Peace Memorial Park; while the main commercial district lies to the east.

Past and Present

"Summer grass
All that remains
Of warriors' dreams."

Haiku composed by the Japanese poet Basho (1644–1694)
on seeing the grave of the warrior Yoshitsune

The Japanese traditionally date the foundation of their nation in 660 B.C., when the legendary emperor Jimmu ascended the throne. They believed that Jimmu was a great-great-grandson of the Shinto sun goddess, Amaterasu. Today we know that although the Japanese islands have been inhabited for thousands of years, the country was in fact united as a nation a thousand years after the legendary date—in about 300 A.D.

The rulers who united the country later became the Japanese emperors. A single dynastic line links the earliest emperors and empresses with the present emperor, Akihito. For much of Japan's history, however, the emperors have been little more than figureheads. Between the 12th and the 19th centuries, actual power lay in the hands of warlords called shoguns and of warriors called samurai. Today the emperor is the head of state of the Japanese democracy that was set up after Japan's defeat in World War II.

Japan's history has been largely shaped by the fact that it is an island nation. Until the mid-20th century, the country suffered no successful foreign invasions. Japanese society and culture, though rooted in those of its overseas neighbor, China, developed largely free of outside influence. In the late 19th and 20th centuries, however, Japan turned outward. It rapidly industrialized and became one of the world's great trading nations.

A ferocious samurai whirls his sword at his enemy. For centuries the powerful warriors known as the samurai held sway over Japanese society.

FACT FILE

● The Japanese emperors are the longest-reigning dynasty of monarchs in the world. The present emperor, Akihito, is 125th in an unbroken line of Japanese rulers that stretches back to the first century B.C.

● Each time a new emperor comes to the throne, a lucky name is chosen for his reign. The reign of the present emperor, Akihito, is known as the Heisei ("fulfillment of peace") era.

● National Foundation Day is celebrated on February 11 every year. The day marks the anniversary of the accession of the first emperor, Jimmu.

EARLY TIMES

No one knows exactly when human beings first settled in Japan. Most historians agree, however, that the earliest peoples arrived some 30,000 years ago, crossing the land bridges that then connected Japan with Siberia and Korea. Some people may also have arrived in boats from Polynesia. These first peoples were hunter-gatherers who used stone tools and weapons.

The Jomōn and Yayoi

About 20,000 years ago, the world climate grew warmer. The sea level rose, and the Sea of Japan was formed, separating the islands of Japan from the mainland of Asia.

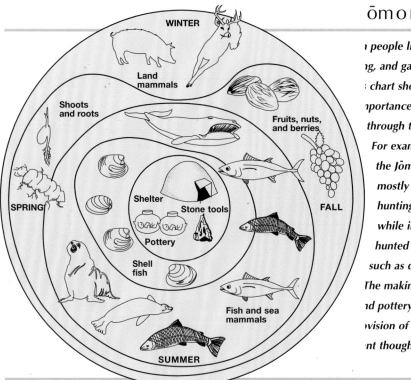

ōmon Year

ɪ people lived by fishing,
ng, and gathering.

chart shows the relative
nportance of each activity
through the seasons.

For example, in summer
the Jōmon survived
mostly by fishing and
hunting sea mammals;
while in winter they
hunted land mammals
such as deer and boar.
The making of tools
nd pottery and the
ɔvision of shelter were
nt thoughout the year.

The islands grew lusher, and from about 10,000 B.C., their inhabitants began to grow vegetables and to fish in the open sea. They also made coiled clay pots, from which their culture gets its modern name—

Jōmon, meaning "cord marked." The Jōmon people wore clothes made from the bark of mulberry trees and wove wicker baskets. They worshiped spirits who inhabited the rivers and mountains of the islands, as well as natural phenomena such as the sun. These beliefs formed the basis of the Japanese religion known as Shinto (*see* box).

The Jōmon shared the Japanese islands with another people, the Ainu, who originally came from north Asia. Gradually the Jōmon and their successors drove the Ainu from the fertile lands of Honshū and into the cold and inhospitable Hokkaidō (*see* p. 50).

During the Yayoi period (300 B.C. to A.D. 300), more settlers reached Kyūshū and western Honshū from China and Korea on the mainland. The newcomers brought new skills: rice-growing, mining, metalworking, weaving, and the use of a wheel to make pottery. People lived in settled communities, growing rice and making bronze and iron tools and weapons. Central and western Japan became a patchwork of small, independent states ruled by clan leaders.

Jōmon pots are the world's oldest datable pottery. The Jōmon people used the pots to cook and store food and also buried them with their dead.

Shinto: Japan's Native Religion

Japan's native religion, Shinto, is very old. It is rooted in the country's landscape and the natural cycle of the seasons. Followers of Shinto worship many spirits, or *kami*, the most important of whom is the sun goddess, Amaterasu.

Throughout the Japanese countryside are simple wooden shrines sacred to the *kami*. The shrines have thatched roofs and are entered by way of a painted wooden gateway, known as a *torii*. Worshipers are always careful to purify themselves before approaching the shrine, rinsing their hands and mouth with clean, fresh water. Sometimes a Shinto priest purifies them by waving a wand of paper strips. Unlike many other religions, Shinto has no holy scripture; instead, its rituals and beliefs have been hallowed by centuries of worship.

神道

The kanji *for Shinto—* shin *and* dō—*mean* "kami [gods]" *and* "way." *Shinto therefore means* "the way of the* kami."

The Ainu: A Threatened Native People

The Ainu were among the earliest inhabitants of Japan. They are in fact several different peoples, and the word Ainu simply means "human being" or "man." Today there are fewer than 14,000 Ainu, who live in villages mostly in the Hidaka district, southeast of Sapporo in Hokkaidō.

The Ainu look very similar to the ethnic Japanese but have their own Ainu language. Over the centuries they have suffered discrimination and today are among the poorest people in Japan. Like other threatened native peoples throughout the world, the Ainu are fighting to preserve their culture.

During the Meiji period (1868–1912), many Ainu customs were banned. Men could not wear earrings, and girls were not allowed to have the traditional blue tattoos around their mouths. The Ainu had to learn to speak and write Japanese. In the 1870s, Ainu people were forced to have Japanese names. When children went to school, they could not study in their own language.

Today only the Ainu elders remember and recite the old epic poems, or *yukar*. These were not written down—people learned them by listening to others reciting Ainu poetry, song, and history. The Ainu and Japanese languages sound quite different. For example, in Ainu "spring" is *sak*, while in Japanese it is *haru*. Sometimes Japanese visitors to Hokkaidō find it hard to pronounce Ainu place-names.

In 1997 the Japanese government passed a law that aims to protect Ainu culture for future generations.

THE FIRST EMPERORS

The period of Japanese history between about A.D. 300 and 710 is known as the Kofun period. The name originates from the great mounds of earth and stone, called *kofun* (literally "old tombs"), which marked the graves of clan chiefs. Today the largest known *kofun* is that of the emperor Nintoku, which can be found on the Osaka Plain. The mound is shaped like a keyhole and covers some 500 acres (200 h). Originally the followers of clan leaders were killed and buried with them to serve their leaders in the afterlife; later, large clay statues of warriors, priests, and horses called *haniwa* were put around the mounds.

Soon after A.D. 300, the head of the Yamato clan from the Osaka Plain, became the most powerful chief. Over the next 250 years, the Yamato leaders gradually unified Japan and eventually took the title of *tennō* (literally "heavenly sovereign"), or emperor. People believed that the emperors were living gods, descended from the goddess Amaterasu. Modern emperors of Japan trace their ancestry back to this clan.

Chinese Influence

During the sixth century, the Buddhist religion reached Japan from Korea and China, bringing with it a strong Chinese influence. Japanese people adopted many aspects of Chinese culture, including

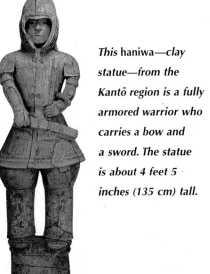

This haniwa—*clay statue—from the Kantō region is a fully armored warrior who carries a bow and a sword. The statue is about 4 feet 5 inches (135 cm) tall.

Early imperial Japan was based in the cities of central Honshū.

Early Japan

These kanji *signify* "Buddha" *and* "teaching" *and together mean the* "teaching of Buddha"*—Buddhism.*

its writing system and calendar. From 593 to 622, Prince Shōtoku (574–622) ruled as regent for a young empress. He built many Buddhist temples and adopted Chinese ideas that increased the power of the emperor.

It was Shōtoku, too, who first referred to Japan as the "Land of the Rising Sun," in a letter to the Chinese emperor. He referred to China as the "Land of the Setting Sun," implying that he considered Japan to be China's equal. The Japanese people still revere Shōtoku today, and his likeness appears on the 10,000-yen bank bill.

The Nara and Heian Periods

In 710 the empress Gemmei founded a new capital at Heijō-kyō, now called Nara. Like Kyōto the city was modeled on the capital of the Chinese emperors, Chang'an (present-day Xi'an), in a gridlike layout. During this era—called the Nara period—Japanese artists created beautiful sculptures of the Buddha, and architects built elegant temples in the Chinese style in which to house them.

Buddhism in Japan

The Buddhist religion developed in India, where its first teacher was Siddhartha Gautama (about 563–483 B.C.)—the Buddha, or "enlightened one." He taught that to achieve happiness human beings had to suppress their Earthly desires. His ideas spread quickly throughout Asia. Different schools, or interpretations, of Buddhism emerged, often as the religion came into contact with different cultures.

Buddhism reached Japan by way of China in the sixth century A.D. At this time, Prince Shōtoku built temples and monasteries and wrote studies on

Buddhist texts. For this reason, the Japanese consider Shōtoku to be the father of Japanese Buddhism. However, Buddhism did not supplant Japan's native religion, Shinto, and often Shinto and Buddhist shrines stood side by side.

Over the centuries, many kinds of Buddhism have developed. Zen Buddhism emphasizes the importance of meditation in achieving salvation. The Jōdo (Pure Land) school teaches that believers have only to recite a simple prayer to Amida—another name for the Buddha.

As the influence of Buddhism grew, the priests became very powerful. In 794 Emperor Kammu decided to move his capital away from Nara because the priests had too much influence over the court. He built a new capital at Heiankyō, later known as Kyōto (*see* pp. 42–43). The Heian period, named after the new capital, was a time of peace and prosperity that lasted nearly 400 years.

During the ninth century, the Japanese broke off relations with China and began to develop their own culture. Japan evolved its own system of writing and produced literature written mainly by women (*see* p. 96). During the Heian period, real power lay not with the emperor but in the hands of a noble family called the Fujiwara. Over the next 300 years, the power of the Fujiwara increased as the clan established large estates throughout western and central Japan.

The Rise of the Shoguns

The peaceful Heian period ended in the 1160s, when civil war broke out between two rival clans, the Minamoto, also called the Genji, and the Taira. In 1185 the Minamoto family under its chiefs, Yoritomo (1147–1181) and his brother, Yoshitsune, won a sea victory over the Taira. After his triumph, Yoritomo made his capital at Kamakura, on the southern coast of Honshū. Jealousy drove Yoshitsune to commit suicide.

Although the imperial capital remained at Kyōto, it was Yoritomo who ruled Japan. In every province there was a military governor called a *shugo*, all of whom reported to Yoritomo in Kamakura. In 1192 the emperor gave Yoritomo the new title of shogun, which means "supreme general." The rule of the shoguns, called the shogunate in English, continued for nearly 700 years.

The first shogun, Minamoto Yoritomo, was a ruthless and cruel ruler. Later, many plays and stories were written about Yoritomo and his handsome, charming brother, Yoshitsune.

53

SHOGUNS AND SAMURAI

The period between the 12th and the 16th centuries was troubled and violent, as rival clan chiefs, known as *daimyō*, fought one another to win power. These lords were backed by armies of warriors called samurai (*see box opposite*). The emperors fought back, rising against the shoguns in 1221 and again in 1333. They failed to regain control of the country, although the shoguns always claimed to govern in the name of the emperor.

The Mongol Invasions

At the end of the 13th century, Japan was threatened by a foreign enemy. The great Mongol warlord Kublai Khan (1214–1294) had conquered huge swaths of Asia, including China, and founded a mighty empire. In 1274 he launched a naval attack on Japan. Before he could land, however, the weather came to the rescue of the Japanese. The captains of the ships that had brought the Khan's troops thought that a typhoon was coming and convinced the Mongol leader to withdraw. The Japanese hurriedly fortified their sea defenses.

In 1281 Kublai Khan tried again, backed by a huge army of 150,000 soldiers. This time the Mongol fleet landed in Hakata Bay, Kūyshū, and fierce fighting broke out. The Japanese were hopelessly outnumbered. All seemed lost when a sudden typhoon wrecked many of the Khan's ships. The Japanese believed that their prayers for help had been answered and called the typhoon a *kamikaze*, or "wind of the *kami* [gods]." Heartened, they launched a counterattack on the Mongols and inflicted massive losses on the invaders.

The Mongol Invasions

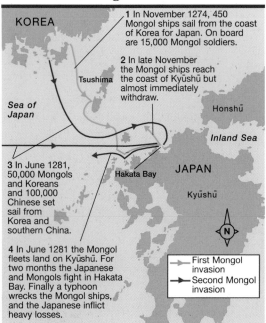

1 In November 1274, 450 Mongol ships sail from the coast of Korea for Japan. On board are 15,000 Mongol soldiers.

2 In late November the Mongol ships reach the coast of Kyūshū but almost immediately withdraw.

3 In June 1281, 50,000 Mongols and Koreans and 100,000 Chinese set sail from Korea and southern China.

4 In June 1281 the Mongol fleets land on Kyūshū. For two months the Japanese and Mongols fight in Hakata Bay. Finally a typhoon wrecks the Mongol ships, and the Japanese inflict heavy losses.

KOREA

Tsushima

Sea of Japan

Honshū

Inland Sea

Hakata Bay · JAPAN

Kyūshū

N

→ First Mongol invasion
→ Second Mongol invasion

The great Mongol leader Genghis Khan led two invasion forces against Japan from China and Korea. Both attempts were unsuccessful, however. The first foreign occupation of Japan did not occur until the 20th century, after the end of World War II.

The Samurai

The samurai were warriors hired by lords to fight their wars and protect their lands. Expert in fighting with the lance, bow, and sword, the samurai swore to defend their master and were expected to die rather than surrender. To avoid disgrace a samurai warrior committed a kind of ritual suicide properly called *seppuku* or, more commonly, *hara-kiri*. The samurai committing *seppuku* stabbed himself in the stomach, while a servant stood by to strike off his head.

The samurai did no work but were supported by taxes paid to their lord by peasants. The samurai followed a strict code of conduct called *bushidō* ("the way of the warrior"). They were expected to be self-disciplined and loyal. They also had to show generosity and kindness to the poor but had the right to take the life of a social inferior who insulted him.

The privileges and duties of being a samurai were passed from father to son. Gradually the samurai came to form a separate class, or caste. They also developed a special way of dressing. Only a samurai had the right to carry a sword. He wore his hair tied back in a top-knot and with his brow and crown shaved bare.

When not fighting, a samurai wore simple clothes. In battle, however, samurai wore elaborate suits of armor like those shown here. (The smaller suit was made for presentation to a samurai boy when he came of age at about 14.) Samurai rode on horseback and carried a bow and arrows and two swords.

During the peaceful Edo period (1603–1868), the samurai did little to earn their keep. Many samurai became *rōnin*, or warriors without masters, and led a precarious life of duels and daredevilry. The samurai developed their fighting skills into ritual arts, which became the basis for martial arts such as judo and aikido. They also practiced *kendō* (Japanese swordfighting) and *kyudō* (archery). The samurai class was abolished in the late 19th century.

The Age of Civil Wars

In 1336 a samurai lord called Ashikaga Takauji (1304–1358) seized power from the Minamoto family and became shogun. The Ashikaga family governed for over 200 years, but the last century of their rule was marked by violence. The period from the mid-15th century to the mid-16th is known as the Age of Civil Wars. The *daimyō* plotted and fought one another to gain land and power, and the central government in Kyōto was too weak to stop them.

Despite all the bloodshed, this was a golden age for arts and crafts. The textiles, ceramics, screen paintings, and lacquerware of this time are considered the finest in Japanese history. Many of the practices that are now considered typically Japanese were established at this time, such as *nō* drama (*see* p. 97), flower arranging (*ikebana*), and the tea ceremony (*see* p. 112). Some of Kyōto's most beautiful gardens were laid out at this time (*see* p. 99).

In the late 16th century, two powerful shoguns tried to reunify Japan under their control. Oda Nobunaga (1534–1582) was a fierce general and a great patron of the arts. In 1585 Toyotomi Hideyoshi (1536–1598) followed in Oda's footsteps. He defeated the other Japanese warlords and even tried to win territory on the Asian mainland. In 1592 and again in 1597, he invaded Korea but was driven back both times.

During the Age of Civil Wars, daimyō families fought each other for supreme power in Japan. The map below shows the various families and their territories.

The Civil Wars

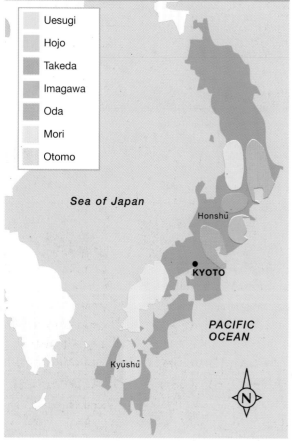

Uesugi
Hojo
Takeda
Imagawa
Oda
Mori
Otomo

Sea of Japan

Honshū

KYOTO

PACIFIC
OCEAN

Kyūshū

N

During the peaceful Edo period, the Japanese nobility enjoyed a life of ease and luxury. At court they wore clothes of gold-embroidered silk, and in their spare time, they practiced arts such as calligraphy ("beautiful writing"), landscape gardening, and growing miniature trees (bonsai). In this screen painting, aristocrats stroll through the streets of Kyōto, the home city of the Japanese imperial family from 764 to1868.

THE EDO PERIOD

In 1603 a warlord called Tokugawa Ieyasu (1542–1616) became shogun. Ieyasu was a clever statesman, determined to control all of Japan. He set up his military capital at Edo (now called Tokyo; *see* p. 33–35), which at this time was little more than a fishing village. Ieyasu set about transforming Edo into a large, busy city. He rebuilt its tumbledown castle, dug canals, and laid out roads. He built no defensive walls, but instead relied on numerous blind alleys and gates that were designed to hinder and confuse invaders.

Ieyasu established an orderly and carefully controlled political system. He divided Japan into 250 domains, each ruled by a *daimyō* who had sworn an oath of loyalty to the shogun. The *daimyō* also had to spend a part of the year in Edo. Iayesu cleverly realized that the *daimyō*

By 1725, Edo had a population of 1,300,000, comprising some 650,000 samurai, 50,000 priests, and 600,000 commoners.

57

would be far too busy making long journeys to and from Edo to be able to hatch any plots against him. Ieyasu also set up a rigid social hierarchy, with four classes. At the top were the samurai. Below them came the farmers, then the craftsmen, and last the merchants or traders. Women were in the same class as their husbands. Strict rules controlled where people in each group lived, the clothes they wore, and even the food they ate.

Using this system the Tokugawa family were able to rule Japan for over 250 years. During their rule, known as the Edo period, peace reigned and the cities grew and prospered. The arts, too, flourished. The period saw the birth of *haiku* poetry, *kabuki* drama, and wood-block printmaking (*see* pp. 95–98).

> "The class of merchants…is very extensive and rich… although their profession is not respected, their wealth is. The commercial spirit of Japan is visible in all the towns and villages."
> Russian visitor to Japan in 1811

The Outside World

During the 16th and early 17th centuries, Japan established limited trade and contact with Western nations. The European powers had been interested in Japan since the 13th century when the Venetian traveler Marco Polo (1254–1324) had returned from China with tales of a rich land to the east. In 1543 Portuguese ships reached Japan, bringing with them the first guns that the Japanese had ever seen.

In the early 1600s, the Tokugawa rulers began to fear that trade with foreign countries might lead to invasion by one of the Western nations. The government decided to cut all links with the outside world. New laws decreed that no Japanese could leave Japan and no foreigners could enter.

Christianity in Japan

Soon after the arrival of the first European ships in Japan, the Spanish Catholic priest Francis Xavier (1506–1552) landed on Kyūshū and began to preach the Christian faith. Over the next hundred years, Spanish and Portuguese missionaries continued his work and converted thousands of Japanese people.

The Japanese met the new religion with suspicion and sometimes violence. In 1597, for example, 26 foreign priests and Japanese converts were crucified. The persecution of Christians reached a peak in 1637 when the Tokugawas ruthlessly crushed a Christian-led rebellion. Until the end of the 19th century, Japanese Christians had to worship in secret.

Foreign sailors shipwrecked on the coasts were killed, and Western books were banned. During this period of isolation, which lasted over 200 years, the only Europeans permitted to enter Japanese waters were Dutch traders, who were allowed to dock at Nagasaki just once a year.

Japan's policy of isolation was called *sakoku* ("closed country").

Mathew Perry in Japan

By the mid-1800s, the Western countries wanted to renew trade with Japan. In 1853 an American fleet of four ships, under the command of Matthew Perry (1794–1858), sailed into Edo Bay. Perry issued a demand that Japan begin trading with the United States and then sailed away, promising to return the following year. In 1854 the Tokugawa government finally signed a friendship and trade treaty with the United States. Similar agreements with Great Britain, Holland, Russia, and France followed.

The changes helped bring about an end to the rule of the Tokugawa. Soon powerful warlords were plotting to overthrow the shogunate and restore the emperor to power. They criticized the Tokugawa for the terms of the treaties, which were generally unfavorable to Japan. After the death of Emperor Komei in 1867, the warlords forced the shogun Tokugawa Yoshinobu to resign and made the 16-year-old emperor Meiji head of state. Because the emperor began to rule the country again, this new era was known as the Meiji Restoration.

This wood-block print shows the arrival of Commodore Perry in Edo Harbor in 1853. The appearance of Perry's "black ship" was a turning point in Japanese history.

IMPERIAL RULE

During the reign of Emperor Meiji (1868–1912), Japan was transformed from a feudal society into a modern industrial nation. The Meiji government looked to the West for inspiration. Japanese leaders were sent to Europe and the United States to learn Western ways, and students went to study at overseas universities. Foreign advisors were invited to Japan to help reform the education and legal systems, transform communications, and set up new industries. The Japanese called the new foreign settlers *gai-koku-jin* (literally "outside-country-people"). The term is still applied to tourists today in a shortened form—*gaijin*.

In 1889 the first Japanese constitution established a parliament of two houses called the Diet (*see* pp. 71–73). The samurai warrior class was abolished and replaced by a modern army and navy. An efficient telegraph system and a railroad network were built up, and modern industries were founded. In the space of less than 50 years, Japan became an advanced, modern country. Backed by a strong army and navy, Japan now set its sights on becoming a powerful force in the Far East.

This wood-block print shows Japan's first railroad, which ran from Tokyo to the port of Yokohama. One frequent U.S. visitor to Tokyo was astonished by the changes that the capital had undergone: " Tokyo is so modernized that I scarcely recognize it...carriages numerous...soldiers all uniformed...new bridges span the canal...Old Yedo [Edo] has passed away forever."

Right: *These are the kanji for the Meiji period.*

The Growth of the Japanese Empire

In 1894 Japan went to war with China over Korea, which both countries wanted to take over. Although China was a much larger country, Japan quickly won the war. The peace treaty with China gave Japan not only some territory in Korea but also the Chinese island of Taiwan.

In 1904 Japan went to war again, this time with Russia, with whom it disputed control of Manchuria, an area in northern China that bordered Russia. Japan wanted Manchuria's rich natural resources, especially its coal and iron ore, for its new industries. The Russian land forces were beaten and at the Battle of Tsu-shima Island, Admiral Heihachiro Togo sank 35 out of 38 Russian ships. The peace treaty with Russia gave Japan overall control in Korea and southern Manchuria.

At its height in 1942, the Japanese empire stretched from the fog-bound Sakhalin Island in the north to the sun-soaked Pacific Islands of the south.

The Japanese Empire, 1900–1945

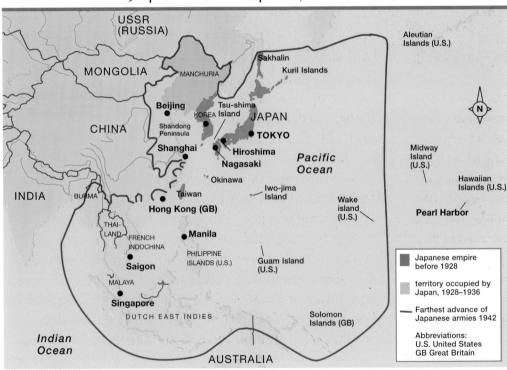

Emperor Meiji died in 1912 and was succeeded by Emperor Taisho, who reigned until 1926. Earlier, in 1902, Japan had made an alliance with Great Britain. When World War I began in 1914, Japan entered the war as Britain's ally, against Germany. Japan took the opportunity to seize Germany's Pacific Islands and Germany's holdings on the Shandong Peninsula.

The 1920s and 1930s were a very troubled time for Japan. In 1923 the Great Kanto Earthquake devastated the Tokyo region and killed more than 100,000 people.

The worldwide economic depression of the early 1930s badly affected Japanese industry. The international price of raw silk—an important Japanese export—fell by two-thirds. Unemployment rose by three million, and there was widespread poverty and disease. Nevertheless, this was also a period that saw new business ideas and opportunities. Many Japanese businesses that are now world-famous were set up at this time, including the Toyota and Nissan automobile corporations and the Fuji film company.

The Great Kanto Earthquake of 1923 virtually flattened the port of Yokohama and much of Tokyo as well. The tremors and the fires that followed killed more than 100,000 people and injured another 50,000. Some three million homes were destroyed across the Kanto Plain.

Growing Ambitions

During the 1930s a growing tide of nationalism swept Japan. The nationalists—many of whom were soldiers in the Japanese army—believed that the Japanese government was weak and corrupt. They wanted to reassert the traditional values of the samurai—patriotism, loyalty, and selflessness—and to stand up to the Western powers.

Many Japanese people supported the army leaders, who believed that Japan needed, and should seize, more territory in order to expand and prosper. In 1931 the Japanese army invaded Manchuria, which had come under Chinese rule in 1907. The Japanese set up a new "puppet" state called Manchukuo, controlled by Japan. The League of Nations, an international organization that aimed at promoting world peace, condemned the move, and Japan left the league.

Right: These are the kanji for the Shōwa ("radiant peace") period, which began in 1926 when Emperor Hirohito came to the throne.

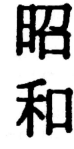

昭
和

The nationalist movement continued to gain support. In 1932 nationalists assassinated Japan's prime minister, Tsuyoshi Inukai, because he opposed the army's ambitions. Army leaders gained more and more control over the government. They began to talk of unifying all of eastern Asia under Japanese rule. A year later, Japan went to war with China, and by 1938 Japanese forces occupied a large part of northeastern China.

The War in the East

At the end of the 1930s, Japan formed alliances with Germany and Italy, both of which were ruled by extreme nationalist dictators. When World War II broke out in 1939, Japan sided with its allies against Britain and France. In 1940 Japan seized the chance to invade French territories in Indochina—the area between India and China.

In 1941 Hideki Tojo, a general with strong anti-American views, became prime minister. Relations between the United States and Japan became increasingly hostile. The United States banned all exports to Japan, including supplies of oil, iron, and steel. Japan hit back, making surprise bombing raids on American military bases in the Pacific, at Pearl Harbor in Hawaii, on Guam and Wake islands, and in the Philippines. It was these attacks that brought the United States into World War II.

During 1941 and early 1942, Japan won dramatic victories. Soon Japanese forces occupied a vast area stretching from Burma and Malaya in the west to the Solomon Islands in the east, and north almost to the Aleutian Islands, which are part of Alaska.

The Japanese air attack on Pearl Harbor on December 7, 1941, sank or damaged eight U.S. battleships. The United States lost some 2,300 men in the attack.

Kamikaze Pilots

In 1944 Vice Admiral Takijiro Onishi came up with an extraordinary idea. Japanese pilots were to fly suicide missions, deliberately crashing their planes into American ships to damage and sink them. Onishi realized that it would be hard to stop the planes because they would have to be destroyed completely before they reached the ship.

The pilots, who flew the missions, were all volunteers. They became known as *kamikaze*, meaning "divine wind," after the typhoon that destroyed the Mongol invasion fleet in 1281

Before each flight a *kamikaze* pilot imitated an old samurai custom and tied a special cloth round his head or arm. The cloth was often decorated with a rising sun, a symbol of Japan. Knowing that there was a good chance that they would not come back, the pilots also gave away their personal belongings to friends and wrote farewell letters.

The *kamikaze* attacks were very destructive, as the planes were often packed with explosives. Sometimes two or more planes would crash into an American warship, setting it on fire. In the fighting at Okinawa, a *kamikaze* force of 1,815 planes sank 32 American ships, killing 5,000 sailors. Half the Japanese planes were lost.

The tide of war began to turn against Japan in June 1942 when the United States won the Battle of Midway. American experts had succeeded in cracking secret Japanese military codes, and four Japanese aircraft carriers were sunk. By 1945 the United States had begun to bomb factories and cities on the Japanese mainland. Tokyo and other major cities were firebombed and nearly burned to the ground, although the historic city of Kyōto was spared. American forces invaded Japanese territory on the islands of Iwo-jima and Okinawa. Despite the bitter fighting, Japan would not surrender.

To avoid the huge American casualties that would likely result from fighting on the Japanese mainland, the United States decided to use a devastating new weapon, the atomic bomb. On August 6, 1945, the first atomic bomb was dropped on the city of Hiroshima. Three days later another bomb struck Nagasaki (*see* pp. 66–67).

On August 14 Emperor Hirohito surrendered on behalf of the his people. In a radio broadcast, the emperor infomed his people of their country's defeat (*see* box). Japan was forced to accept that it was conquered for the first time in its history.

Surrender and Occupation

Under the terms of the surrender, Japan lost all its territories on the Asian mainland and its islands in the Pacific, including Taiwan. Japan's land area was restricted to its four main islands and smaller surrounding islands. The Japanese also had to submit to a military occupation by the Allied forces—mainly American servicemen—under the command of General Douglas MacArthur (1880–1964).

The aim of the Allied occupation was to end Japan's military ambitions and establish democracy. The Allies also wanted to reduce the power of the *zaibatsu*, the large corporations behind Japanese industry that had supported the war. The army, navy, and airforce were abolished, and military leaders were tried for war crimes. Some, including former prime minister Hideki Tojo, were executed.

In 1947 a new constitution went into effect, declaring that Japan's sovereignty lay with the Japanese people, not with the emperor. It added that the emperor was not

"Long Live the Emperor!"

When the voice of Emperor Hirohito was broadcast on the radio at the end of World War II, it was the first time that most Japanese had ever heard the emperor speak. It was a strange moment for people who believed that the emperor was a god. In fact, some people may not even have understood everything Hirohito said because some words he used were older forms of the Japanese language, used only at the emperor's court.

Since then, much of the mystique surrounding Japan's emperors has disappeared. Nevertheless, today the royal family is still highly respected. As a representative of the nation and a symbol of the unity of the Japanese people, the emperor attends official ceremonies and signs decisions made by the Diet, or parliament.

The Hiroshima Blast

During World War II, the U.S. military repeatedly bombarded Japan's cities. In three days of bombing raids in March 1945, for example, Tokyo was burned to the ground. More than 100,000 people were killed and thousands more left homeless. By the summer of 1945, hardly a city in Japan was left unscathed.

Remarkably, until August 1945, the city of Hiroshima (*see* pp. 44–45) had not been targeted by the American bombing. On the morning of August 6, 1945, the city's good luck changed. At 8.15 A.M., as people made their way to work, the sky above the city erupted into a huge fireball. The U.S. military had dropped the first atomic bomb (A-bomb) used in warfare.

The Americans first developed the A-bomb in 1944–1945. The weapon relied on the discovery that when the nucleus of a uranium or plutonium atom is artificially split, a huge explosion of energy—light, heat, and radioactivity—is released. The first bomb was tested only a few weeks before the Hiroshima explosion—at a desert site in New Mexico.

The Hiroshima bomb—nicknamed "Little Boy"—had the destructive power of 15,000 tons of TNT. It exploded 1,900 feet (580 m) above the city center, creating a huge fireball half a mile (1 km) in diameter. In a moment, the blast consumed the city—70,000 buildings and 80,000 people were destroyed in the first few moments. The heat was so fierce that all that remained of some victims was their shadows seared into the rubble.

At the time, the inhabitants of Hiroshima did not know anything about the A-bomb or about

The pilot of the Enola Gay waves from the cockpit on the day of the Hiroshima blast—August 6, 1945.

its devastating power. At first, many thought the city had been struck by ordinary bombs. Only gradually did it become clear that they were the victims of a new and terrifying weapon.

In his famous book about the first A-bomb, *Hiroshima*, American writer John Hersey tells the story of six people who lived through the blast and its aftermath. One woman was at home with her children when the bomb exploded. Hersey reports what happened to her next:

"Everything flashed whiter than any white she had ever seen. She did not notice what happened to the man next door; the reflex of a mother set her in motion toward her children. She had taken a single step (the

house was 1,350 yards, or three-quarters of a mile, from the center of the explosion) when something picked her up and she seemed to fly into the next room over the raised sleeping platform, pursued by parts of her house.

"Timbers fell around her as she landed, and a shower of tiles pummelled her; everything became dark, for she was buried... She heard a child cry, "Mother, help me!" and saw her youngest—Myeko, the five year old—buried up to her breast and unable to move. As Mrs. Nakamura started frantically to claw her way toward the baby, she could see or hear nothing of her other children."

By the end of 1945, 60,000 more people had died from burns, wounds, and radiation sickness. Even today, many people continue to live with the injuries and trauma that resulted both from the Hiroshima blast and from the second bomb blast that devastated Nagasaki. The Japanese call the survivors of the atomic blasts the *hibakusha*.

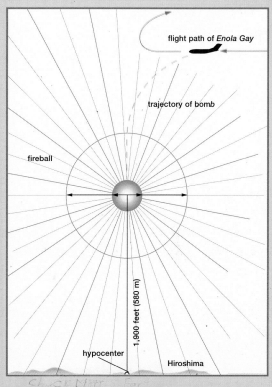

The Hiroshima bomb exploded high above the city, creating a huge fireball that incinerated the city below. The point on the ground directly below a nuclear explosion is called the hypocenter.

The A-bomb blast virtually flattened the city of Hiroshima for an area with a radius of a mile and a half (2.4 km).

a god, as had been previously claimed. Economic and land reforms were also made, aimed at rebuilding Japan's shattered industries and ruined cities.

The Allied occupation was a humiliating blow for Japan, but it did not last long. By 1949, General MacArthur could announce that its main aims had been achieved. When war broke out in Korea in 1950, Japan helped to supply the United Nations (UN) forces with weapons, tools, and vehicles. This provided a kickstart for Japanese industry and helped Japan take its first step to becoming an ally of the United States. The Allied occupation ended officially in April 1952, although American forces remained in Japan. In 1956 Japan became a member of the UN.

DEMOCRATIC JAPAN

From the 1950s to the 1970s, there was an "economic miracle" in Japan. A defeated country, with many of its major industrial centers destroyed, managed to become one of the world's great industrial nations (*see* pp. 75–89) and most stable democracies.

Many reasons lay behind this rapid recovery. The Allies helped Japan to import new technology cheaply, so the country did not need to spend money on research. With no army or navy, Japan spent little money on defense. Factories were rebuilt and the latest equipment was installed. Japan's new industries concentrated on producing goods that would be needed throughout the world. The workers were well trained and highly skilled. They united behind their employers to work long hours, and everyone pulled together to put the country back on its feet.

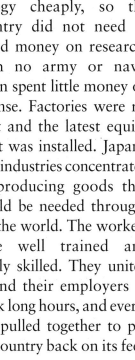

Japan's automobile industry was at the heart of the postwar "economic miracle." Companies such as Nissan and Toyota led the way in exporting well-built and affordable vehicles around the world. By 1970, Japan was producing more than three million automobiles every year.

In 1960 the new prime minister, Hayato Ikeda, announced a national plan that aimed to double the country's income within ten years. The plan was so successful that the average income in Japan doubled only four years later. During the 1960s and 1970s, the country prospered and Japan became a nation of consumers. By 1964, 90 percent of Japanese homes possessed the "three treasures"—a television, a refrigerator, and a washing machine. In the same year, Japan hosted the Olympic Games, which helped establish a new positive image of the country in the world.

When the Arab–Israeli War of 1973 caused oil prices to rise suddenly around the world, Japanese industry suffered, like that of many developed countries. Japan moved away from heavy industries that relied on fuel and raw materials to concentrate on light industries such as electronics. When the second "oil shock" came in 1979, Japan was much less affected. In the late 1960s and early 1970s, the United States returned Japan's Pacific island territories, the Bonin and the southern Ryūkyū islands, including Okinawa. The Soviet Union, however, did not return the most southerly of the Kuril Islands—Simushir, Urup, Iturip, and Kunasir—near the coast of Hokkaidō, which it had seized at the end of World War II.

By the 1980s, Japan was the world's third-largest exporter, after the United States and West Germany. Japan invested abroad, opening its first automobile plants in Tennessee and in Britain. The program of foreign investment continued through the 1980s, as the value of the Japanese yen continued to rise. By the end of the decade, Japan produced one-third of the world's automobiles and ships and two-thirds of its electronic goods.

The Kuril Islands are a chain of 56 volcanic islands that stretch from Kamchatka to Hokkaidō. Geographically, the islands look like a link between Japan and Russia; politically, however, they have driven the nations apart.

The Kuril Islands

69

平成

In 1989 Emperor Hirohito died and was succeeded by his son Akihito. This began a new era, known as Heisei, which means "the fulfillment of peace." These are the kanji *for Heisei.*

After World War II, Japan protected its industries by imposing tight controls on imported goods, ensuring that Japanese people always bought Japanese products. In the 1970s and 1980s, however, the United States and other countries protested against this system.

Slowdown and Instability

By the end of the 1980s, the rate of economic growth was slowing in Japan. These new difficulties brought about political change at home. In 1993 the Liberal Democratic Party, which had been in power since 1955, was defeated, and a new eight-party coalition government (a combination of political groups) led by Prime Minister Morihiro Hosokawa took control.

Japan entered a period of instability and uncertainty. Unemployment was on the rise, and the economy was threatened by the collapse of several big banks and companies. To make matters worse, a huge earthquake struck Kōbe in January 1995. The disaster leveled whole neighborhoods and killed more than 5,000 people. A couple of months later, a religious cult carried out a poison gas attack on the Tokyo subway.

Abroad Japan was increasingly criticized for not playing a more active role in peacekeeping missions around the world. Japan's answer was that its constitution did not allow it to take part in wars, and that it gave huge sums of money in foreign aid. In 1992, however, Japanese troops took part in a United Nations (UN) peacekeeping mission in Cambodia, and Japan agreed to provide UN forces with more support.

The Yakuza

The *yakuza* are a powerful criminal class in Japan, whose influence reaches throughout society, from big business and government to the hospitals and real estate. There are some 90,000 *yakuza* members in Japan, each of whom belongs to one of seven major networks. The largest of these is in Kōbe and has a membership of 20,000. Like the Italian or U.S. Mafia, the *yakuza* have a fierce code of honor. A member caught breaking the code is often subjected to violent punishment. Members often have tattoos that cover their whole body. Many Japanese worry that the power of the *yakuza* could undermine democracy.

JAPAN'S GOVERNMENT

Japan is a parliamentary democracy. The emperor is the ceremonial head of state, but since 1947, power has been in the hands of the Japanese people. The constitution guarantees its citizens many rights, including freedom of speech and of religion. May 3—the date of the proclamation of the constitution—is celebrated every year with a public holiday.

Voting is considered very important in Japan. Everyone aged 20 and over has the right to vote. Women have had the vote since 1947. On January 15 each year, local town halls hold a civic ceremony to honor those who have reached voting age.

Japan's parliament, called the *Kokkai* (Diet), passes laws and controls taxes. The Diet

The 1947 Constitution

The American lawyers who drew up the Japanese constitution of May 1947 modeled it closely on that of the United States. Many of the constitution's articles guarantee fundamental liberties. One article proclaims "All the people should be respected as individuals," thereby abolishing the old legal code that had given husbands unequal rights over their wives. One article, however, is unique, found in no other constitution in the world: "…the Japanese people forever renounce war as a sovereign right of the nation and the threat or use of force as a means of settling international disputes."

The National Diet Building—home of Japan's parliament— is in Tokyo, west of the Imperial Palace. The building is modeled on the U.S. Senate Building. To the left is the House of Representatives and to the right is the House of Councillors.

Japan's principal
prime ministers
since 1945 have
been:
**Yoshida Shigeru
(1946–1947 and
1948–1954)**
**Kishi Nobusuke
(1957–1960)**
**Ikeda Hayato
(1960–1964)**
**Sato Eisaku
(1964–1972)**
**Nakasone Yasuhiro
(1982–1987)**
**Miyazawa Kiichi
(1991–1993)**
**Obuchi Keizo
(1998–)**

has two houses. The *Shūgiin* (House of Representatives),
the more powerful house, is made up of 500 members,
who are elected for four years. The *Sangiin* (House of
Councillors) has 252 members, elected for six years. The
head of government (prime minister) is chosen by the Diet
and is usually the leader of the party with the majority.
The prime minister appoints the *Naikaku*, or Cabinet, of
ministers. In turn, the Cabinet appoints the chief justice
and 14 senior justices who make up the *Saikō Saibansho*,
or Supreme Court. The government offices are situated in
the Kasumigaseki district of Tokyo.

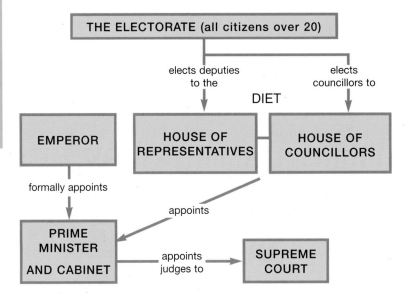

*Japan's system of
government is like a
mixture of the British
and U.S. systems.
The emperor, like
the British king
or queen, is the
symbolic head of
the nation but has
no real power. In
common with the
U.S. system, there
are two elected houses,
or democratic bodies.*

In terms of local government, Japan is divided into 47
administrative units, or prefectures (*see* p. 18). Each prefecture has its own elected governor and assembly. Within
each prefecture, each city (*shi*), town (*machi* or *chō*), and
village (*mura*) has its own mayor and local assembly.

Parties and Elections

Japan has numerous political parties. The most successful, however, is the Liberal Democratic Party (LDP; in
Japanese *Jiyu-Minshuto*). This conservative party was
set up in 1955 and remained in power for nearly 40 years.

THE JAPANESE DIET IN 2000

House of Representatives
500 members • Last election 1997• Elections held every 4 years

LDP (Liberal Democratic Party)	52.6%
DPJ (Democratic Party of Japan)	18.4%
New Komeito	9.4%
LP (Liberal Party)	8%
others	11.6%

House of Councillors
252 members • Last election 1998 • Half of members elected every third year for a six-year term

LDP (Liberal Democratic Party)	47.2%
DPJ (Democratic Party of Japan)	16.4%
New Komeito	9.6%
SDP (Social Democratic Party)	8.4%
others	18.4%

The Liberal Democratic Party remains dominant in both houses of the Japanese Diet. The principal party of opposition is the Democratic Party of Japan. In recent years, however, the New Komeito (Clean Government Party) has gained more and more support.

It is popular in rural areas and with business corporations. Other major political parties include the Democratic Party of Japan (DPJ), the Socialist Democratic Party of Japan (SDPJ), New Komeito, and the Japanese Communist Party. Since 1996, the country has been run by a coalition, in which the LDP holds the most seats.

Japanese troops in Cambodia (Kampuchea) wear the blue beret of the United Nations peacekeeping forces.

The Economy

"In all sorts of handicrafts...they are wanting neither proper materials, nor industry and application...they rather exceed all other nations in ingenuity and neatness of

17th-century German visitor to Japan Engelbert Kaempfer

The Japanese economy is one of the strongest in the world. In only a hundred years from the 1870s, Japan grew from a poor, undeveloped country into a rich, industrial nation. Japan emerged from World War II defeated and financially ruined. However, during the 1950s and 1960s, Japanese industry shrewdly reinvested profits into research and development. By the mid-1970s, Japan was filing more patents than the United States.

Today Japan's economic output ranks in the world's top three countries, along with the United States and Germany. With few natural resources, the key to Japan's success is foreign trade. In terms of exports, its strength lies in manufacturing. Japanese automobiles, ships, and consumer goods are sold all over the world. Almost a quarter of Japan's workers are employed in manufacturing and construction. Other major industries include services, transportation, farming, and fishing.

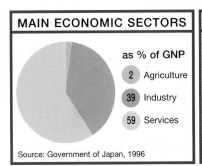

MAIN ECONOMIC SECTORS

as % of GNP

2 Agriculture
39 Industry
59 Services

Source: Government of Japan, 1996

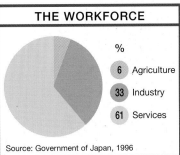

THE WORKFORCE

%

6 Agriculture
33 Industry
61 Services

Source: Government of Japan, 1996

The trading floor at the Tokyo Stock Exchange can be a whirlwind of activity, with traders buying and selling stocks and shares at a frantic pace.

MAIN TRADING PARTNERS

EXPORTS

IMPORTS

%	
27.2	U.S.
7.1	South Korea
6.3	Taiwan
6.2	Hong Kong
5.3	China
5.1	Singapore
42.8	Others

%	
22.7	U.S.
11.6	China
4.6	South Korea
4.4	Indonesia
4.3	Taiwan
4.1	Australia
48.3	Others

Source: Government of Japan, 1996

The vast majority of Japan's trade— both imports and exports—is with the United States. This in part reflects the role played by America in the reconstruction of the Japanese economy after World War II.

TRADE

Japan relies on foreign trade to pay for its imports of fuel, raw materials, and other products. With around 10 percent of the world export market, Japan is a major player in international trade. Its most important partner is the United States, which provides Japan with almost a quarter of its imports, and, in turn, takes some 27 percent of Japanese exports.

Japan also has important trade links with Southeast Asian countries on the shores of the Pacific. Industry in these countries—including Taiwan, South Korea, Singapore, Indonesia, and China—is developing fast. Australia, too, is an important trading partner.

Since the 1980s the value of Japan's exports has exceeded the value of its imports. This results in a net profit known as a trade surplus. In the late 1980s and early 1990s, Japan's trade surplus was the largest in the world. This was partly due to the work of the Ministry of International Trade and Industry (MITI), which supports Japanese industries and funds new research. The MITI also protects Japanese trade by restricting imports—limiting the quantity of goods that can enter Japan and imposing taxes on foreign imports.

Japan's import restrictions apply especially to farm products. For example, the price of Japan's homegrown rice is very expensive, but by law, imports of rice are banned. In recent years, nations such as the United States have objected to this arrangement, which places foreign products at a disadvantage. At one point in the 1980s, Japan's trade surplus with the United States was in excess of $30 billion. Now Japan has agreed to try to reduce its trade surplus by lifting barriers to foreign trade and increasing imports.

MAJOR SECTORS

Japan is one of the most industrialized countries in the world. Along the coasts of Honshū and Kyūshū is a dense network of factories, warehouses, and transportation systems.

Small-scale Farming

Farms occupy only 12 percent of the land in Japan. The rest of the country is too mountainous to farm or is occupied by towns and factories. Because space is tight, farms are very small. A typical Japanese farm covers only about 250 acres (100 ha) compared to an average of 469 acres (190 ha) for each farm in the United States. Crop yields in Japan are high because the land is farmed intensively, using fertilizers and weedkillers. Machines do much of the work. Altogether Japan produces about 70 percent of its food; the rest is imported.

Before World War II, most farmland was owned by wealthy landlords. Tenant farmers worked the land, but up to half of their harvest went to the landlords as rent. After the war, the ownership system was reformed, and small farmers were given help to buy land. Now most farmland is owned by the families that work it.

EXPORTS

IMPORTS

EXPORTS ($bn)	
Motor vehicles	50.7
Office machinery	29.3
Chemicals	28.8
Scientific equipment	17.4
Iron & steel	15.2
Total (inc. others)	410.9

IMPORTS ($bn)	
Mineral fuels	60.6
Agric. products	50.8
Textiles	25.6
Chemicals	23.3
Wood	9.6
Total (inc. others)	349.1

Source: Government of Japan, 1996

Since the 1980s Japan has exported much more than it has imported. The value of its current account balance in 1996 stood at $65.9 billion.

This Japanese farmer is harvesting potatoes. Because arable land is so scarce and fragmented in Japan, fields—and the machinery needed to farm them—are often small-scale.

Farmers make up only 6 percent of the Japanese workforce. Most farmers also have full-time jobs in offices or factories and farm only on weekends. National holidays such as Golden Week in early May coincide with busy periods in the farming year, so farmers can spend time in the fields, planting or harvesting.

Many young people from farming families do not wish to work the land. Instead, they leave country areas to seek better-paid and less back-breaking work in towns and cities. Today, most farmers in Japan are older people, aged 55 and over.

LAND USE

Japan's mountainous inland is densely forested. Croplands are confined to narrow coastal strips.

Cropland

Forest

Pastureland

Rice is by far the most important crop in Japan. It is the staple food and is eaten at nearly every meal. All over Japan, steep, hilly land is cut into steps to make flat terraces that can be planted with crops, or flooded to make paddyfields for rice. In the past, the island of Kyūshū in the south was the main rice-growing region. Now hardier strains of rice have been developed, and most rice is grown on Hokkaidō in the north.

Rice amounts to one-third of Japan's total harvest. Other important crops are wheat, barley, tea, and tobacco. Vegetables and fruits include sweet potatoes, eggplants, sugar beet, radishes, carrots, cabbages, watermelons, strawberries, and tomatoes. Apples and pears are grown in the north, while southern orchards yield tropical fruits such as mandarin oranges, peaches, tangerines, and nectarines.

The island of Hokkaidō is one of the least developed parts of Japan and is an important farming area. The main crops grown here are oats and potatoes. Beef and dairy cattle are raised on grassy pastures. The lowlands around the shores of the Inland Sea in the south of Japan yield many kinds of fruit. On the southern coasts of Kyūshū and Shikoku, the main crop is sweet potatoes.

Traditionally, few animals were reared for meat in Japan because it is against Buddhist principles to kill animals. Today meat has become much more popular. Chickens are reared for eggs and meat, and pigs are raised for pork. Cattle are reared for beef and dairy products. Beef from cattle raised near the city of Kōbe is an expensive delicacy. The cattle are kept underground, fed on beer, and massaged every day.

Forests cover 67 percent of Japan, but the country harvests little of its own timber. Wood is imported from the tropical rain forests of Southeast Asia, which have suffered huge environmental damage as a consequence. Nevertheless, there is growing awareness and concern about the logging of the tropical rain forests in Japan, as in other parts of the world.

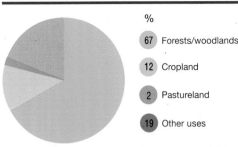

LAND USE

%
67 Forests/woodlands
12 Cropland
2 Pastureland
19 Other uses

Source: Government of Japan

This chart shows the percentages of land given over to various uses.

A Great Fishing Nation

Traditionally, fish forms a main part of the Japanese diet. It is eaten either raw, broiled, or fried. Fishing is a major industry in Japan. The country's fishing fleet is the largest in the world, with more than 400,000 fishing vessels. The fleet cruises the waters of the Indian, Pacific, and Atlantic oceans, also visiting the icy seas of the Arctic

Silk Farming

Central Honshū is famous for its mulberry trees. The leaves are used to feed the larvae (young) of silkworm moths, which are raised on special farms. From its saliva, each silkworm produces silk to make a cocoon, a kind of case that protects it while it changes from a caterpillar into an adult moth. The cocoons are unwound and spun into a thread, which is then woven into silk fabric. Since a cocoon weighs approximately .02 ounces (8 dg), it takes thousands of cocoons to make a few pounds (1 kg) of raw silk. As a material, silk is soft, strong, and warm in cold weather. Japanese silkworms produce 44,000 tons (40,000 t) of silk each year.

Potential buyers inspect frozen tuna during an auction at the Tsukiji Fish Market in Tokyo.

and Antarctic in search of good fishing grounds. Tuna, salmon, pollock, and squid are some of the most important catches. In open waters, fishing boats net cod and sardines. Closer to shore, mackerel and shellfish, such as crabs, shrimps, and clams, are caught. Each year, Japan nets over 13.2 million tons (12 million t) of fish—an eighth of the world's catch.

Environmentalists criticize Japan for its practice of driftnet fishing. Two boats drag a fine net between them, sweeping up everything that lies in their way. The net is usually about 50 feet (15 m) deep and the two boats hauling it can be as much as 30 miles (50 km) apart. The fishermen are aiming to catch tuna, but turtles, dolphins, sharks, and countless other sea creatures get caught up in the nets, too, and are left to die.

In the past, Japan was an important whaling nation. Today, there is an international ban on whaling, though Japanese ships continue to catch some whales for "scientific purposes."

Fish is the major source of protein in the Japanese diet. On average, each person in Japan eats 66 pounds (30 kg) of fish every year.

Many different kinds of fish are farmed in Japan. Carp, trout, and eels are reared inland in ponds and tanks. Tuna and sea bream are farmed in sheltered coastal bays. Seaweed is also harvested on the coasts around Japan for use in Japanese cooking.

Natural Resources

Japan's economic success is all the more remarkable because its natural resources are very limited. Its mines produce copper, lead, limestone, manganese, tin, zinc, gold, and silver, but not in quantities large enough to meet the country's needs. Most of the minerals and metal ores necessary for industry, including large amounts of copper and bauxite, are imported.

Large quantities of iron and coal are used by Japan's iron and steel industry. The country imports iron ore from Australia, Brazil, and India. Japan has coal mines on Hokkaidō and Kyūshū, but they produce only low-grade coal that is expensive to mine. To supply its industries, Japan imports large stocks of coal from Australia, Canada, and the United States.

With only poor-grade coal, Japan lacks the rich deposits of fossil fuels—formed from the remains of animals and plants—needed to meet its energy needs. The main fuel used for generating energy is oil, but the small deposits of oil found on the northwest coast of Honshū meet only a tiny fraction of the country's needs. Once again Japan must import supplies. Oil comes mainly from the Middle East, but also from Southeast Asia, Mexico, and China. Crude oil, together with natural gas, represents a large percentage of the total value of all the goods and raw materials that Japan imports from overseas—some 17 percent in 1996.

Some of Japan's energy needs are met by the nuclear power and hydroelectricity generated by the country's fast-flowing rivers. Japan has more than 40 nuclear power stations (*see* box).

ENERGY SOURCES

%
55.2	Oil and petroleum products
16.4	Coal
12.3	Nuclear
11.3	Natural gas
3.4	Hydroelectricity
1.4	Other

Source: Government of Japan, 1996

Japan depends on fossil fuels such as oil, coal, and gas to meet its energy needs.

Nuclear Power

Japan's decision to build nuclear power plants comes despite protests from many Japanese people. The Japanese have been sensitive to the dangers of nuclear radiation ever since the United States dropped atomic bombs on Hiroshima and Nagasaki during World War II. In 1999, moreover, a nuclear explosion at a uranium-processing plant northeast of Tokyo injured 19 workers. In the future, Japan may rely more on renewable energy sources, such as wind power and geothermal energy.

These women are working on a production line making televisions in a factory near Ōsaka. Sony, Mitsubishi, and Toshiba are world-famous brands of electrical equipment and have pioneered new developments, such as flat-screen TVs and PlayStation.

A Wealth of Manufacturing

Today almost every home in a developed country contains products made in Japan. But the success of Japan's manufacturing industry dates back only 50 years. At the end of World War II, Japan's factories lay in ruins. A government department called the Ministry of International Trade and Industry (MITI) rebuilt factories and encouraged exports.

The steelmaking and shipbuilding industries were the first to be redeveloped in the 1950s. Then came the consumer industries, producing goods such as cameras and cars. In the 1970s Japan switched to lighter industries such as electronics, which relied less on imported materials and more on skilled workers. Recently new industries such as aerospace and biotechnology have also become important.

The success of Japanese manufacturing lies in good management, company loyalty, and hard work. Japanese firms invest large sums in developing new products. Their factories use the latest equipment and technology, including robots.

Today the most important industries in Japan are the automobile industry and electronics. Iron, steel, and shipbuilding are still important, as is the petrochemical industry, which refines oil and makes plastics. Japan is also world-famous for making precision equipment, such as binoculars, watches, and musical instruments, and for cement, textiles, clothing, and ceramics.

Japan's main manufacturing region lies on the southern coast of Honshū, from the western tip of the island east as far as Tokyo. All along the Pacific coast, factories have

MAJOR INDUSTRIES

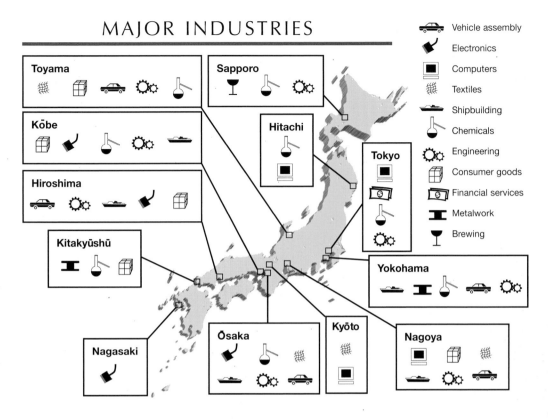

Vehicle assembly
Electronics
Computers
Textiles
Shipbuilding
Chemicals
Engineering
Consumer goods
Financial services
Metalwork
Brewing

Toyama

Sapporo

Kōbe

Hitachi

Hiroshima

Tokyo

Kitakyūshū

Yokohama

Nagasaki

Ōsaka

Kyōto

Nagoya

grown up around ports that receive vital supplies of fuel and raw materials. The regions around Tokyo and Nagoya are known for vehicles, machinery, and chemicals. Ōsaka and Kōbe produce machinery, iron and steel, and chemicals. Kōbe is famous for its shipyards.

Farther west, in the lowlands around the Inland Sea, including northern Shikoku, vehicles, ships, iron, and steel are produced. The Hokuriku region on the west coast of Honshū is famous for textiles and chemicals. Western Kyūshū produces cars and electronic goods.

Japan's iron and steel industries were redeveloped after World War II. The steel is used to make ships, automobiles, machinery, and buildings. Along the Pacific coast, some iron and steel plants have been built on land reclaimed from the sea. The shipbuilding industry also developed from knowledge and skills learned in wartime. The shipyards sprang up near steel mills because they used large quantities of steel. In the 1960s and 1970s,

Most of Japan's industry is found on Honshū island, especially in the Tokyo and Ōsaka regions.

Japanese factories are some of the world's most advanced. Production lines such as this one are monitored by computer and are highly efficient.

Japan built the first supertankers and supplied over half of the world's ships. Today the industry is less important, but still builds 40 percent of the world's ships.

Japan's automobile industry is the largest in the world. With nearly 28 percent of the world market, it outstrips even the United States. When the first Japanese automobiles reached Western countries in the 1960s, they were not considered serious competition. Now Japanese firms produce 8 million automobiles and 7.5 million trucks and buses each year. More than half these vehicles are exported to Europe and North America. The motor industry employs more than five million workers in Japan alone; giant companies such as Mitsubishi, Honda, Toyota, and Nissan employ thousands more in factories worldwide.

The electrical and electronics industry has mainly developed since the 1970s. Now Japanese radios, stereo systems, television sets, video recorders, calculators, fax machines, cameras, and computers are popular all over the world. Japan produces most of the world's industrial robots used in factories, and 80 percent of all microchips—the tiny circuits that run electronic equipment. In the early years of the industry, Japan imported technology from the United States and Europe and used it to develop highly successful products. More recently, products such as the video recorder and the personal stereo were invented in Japan. Now companies are focusing on digital technology, lasers, and fiber optics as well as electronics.

Industrial Pollution

Japan's rapid industrial growth from the 1950s has been achieved at the expense of the environment. Factories belched smoke, soot, and sulfur and nitrogen dioxide into the air. Exhaust fumes from automobiles added lead and toxic gases such as carbon monoxide. By the 1970s, air pollution in some cities was so bad that people had to wear face masks.

Factories also discharged poisonous chemicals such as mercury and cadmium into streams and rivers, polluting water. Between 1956 and 1967, one chemical company discharged waste containing mercury into Minamata Bay in Kyūshū, poisoning the local fish and shellfish. People who ate seafood from the bay became very ill. Up to 20,000 people were affected by "Minamata Disease," and 857 later died. Many suffered severe damage to the nervous system. In the 1970s, people living near Toruku Mine on Kyūshū were poisoned after their drinking water was polluted by arsenic from the mine.

Today Japan's government imposes strict antipollution controls on factories. Automobiles run on leadfree gasoline and are fitted with catalytic converters, to reduce toxic exhaust gases. The air, land, and water in Japan are now much cleaner than they were 20 years ago.

In many areas national parks have been established to protect the environment. Japan also has a good record in recycling materials such as glass and paper.

Working Life

Work dominates life in Japan far more than it does in many developed countries. Most people work six days a week and take only one or two weeks' vacation each year.

In offices and factories, the day begins with workers bowing to each other and singing the company song. Everyone joins in physical exercises before meeting to discuss the day's work. Employees work late and are expected to go out and socialize with coworkers after work. Ambitious executives do not get home much before midnight, and Sunday is the only day when men spend time with their families. Recently, people have begun to recognize the dangers of overwork. After a number of exhausted businessmen dropped dead in the street, the Japanese invented a term for the phenomenon—*karōshi*, meaning "death by overwork."

Unemployment in Japan has traditionally been very low. More recently, however, levels have increased. Among young adults some 6 percent are unemployed.

These Japanese office workers are exercising together before beginning their morning work. Team spirit is very important in Japanese companies. Wearing the same clothes and eating together are thought to improve productivity and create a close-knit community.

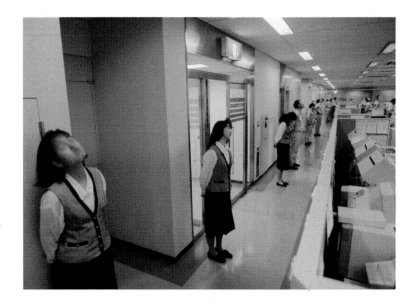

Most visitors to Japan come from the neighboring countries of South Korea and Taiwan.

MAIN OVERSEAS ARRIVALS

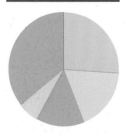

%

26 South Korea

18 Taiwan

14 USA

6 China

36 Others

Source: Government of Japan, 1997

Almost a third of all Japanese workers work for a big company. Employees traditionally join when they leave school and stay with the same company until they retire. There are very few strikes. Employers expect hard work and loyalty. In return the company provides employees with cheap housing in a suburb near the factory. It pays for health care, arranges annual holidays, and even provides scholarships for workers' children. This system, called lifetime employment, is still common in big companies, though recently some firms have been hit by economic difficulties and have had to dismiss personnel.

TRANSPORTATION

Japan's transportation system is extremely efficient. Plans are under way to develop networks of new superhighways, bullet trains, and airports so that any part of Japan can be reached from Tokyo in under 90 minutes.

The Rail Network

Japan's rail network is fast and efficient. The rail network was begun during the Meiji Restoration in the 1870s. Now trains carry 40 percent of travelers in Japan. The Japan Railways Group is the biggest railway operator.

In the 1960s, Japan pioneered high-speed trains. Today's *shinkansen*, or bullet trains, are among the fastest in the world. These services run from Morioka in northern Honshū to Fukuoka in Kyūshū in the west, traveling at speeds of up to 170 miles per hour (275 km/h). Some fast trains are double-deckers. When trains pull into major stations, passengers are already waiting in line on marks painted on the platform. These show the position of the doors of the trains, which always stop in the same spot.

Japan's largest cities all have subway systems. At peak hours the trains are very crowded. Shinjuku Station in Tokyo is one of the busiest in the world. Trains arrive every minute, and officials called *oshiya* (literally, "pushers") stand by to help cram commuters on trains.

In the 1990s, a new kind of train was being developed in Japan. Maglev—an abbreviation of magnetic levitation—trains will be pulled along at speeds of up to 300 miles per hour (480 km/h). A magnet placed on the underside of the train on the track is repelled by others, causing the train to float above the track.

Japan's first subway was built in 1927, in downtown Tokyo. Today there are also subway systems in Ōsaka, Nagoya, Sapporo, Yokohama, Kōbe, Fukuoka, and Kyōto.

This bullet train is crossing a bridge in Ginza, one of Tokyo's busiest districts.

In Japan automobiles drive on the left side of the road.

Busy Roads

Japan has over 620,000 miles (1 million km) of roads. Most roads run north to south, using the flatter ground near the coasts, rather than west to east across the mountains. Superhighways link all the major cities. There are more than 30 million automobiles in Japan and more than 20 million trucks. Most freight goes by road, but driving is not a very efficient means of transportation in Japan for passengers. Fuel is expensive, and the roads are very congested. During peak hours the traffic jams around Tokyo may stretch for 50 miles (80 km) or more. Special boxes by the roadside provide drivers with the latest satellite information about congested routes. Parking in large cities has become a major problem. To register an automobile, drivers must first prove they have somewhere to park it.

Over the last 20 years, a vast network of bridges and tunnels has been built to carry road and rail traffic between Japan's four main islands. In 1998, the longest suspension bridge in the world—the Akashi Kaikyō Bridge—opened, helping link Honshū and Shikoku.

In Kōbe's busy, smoky harbor, industrial wharves, docks, and industrial plants are built on land reclaimed from the sea.

TRANSPORTATION

Japan has a well-organized and highly efficient transportation system. More than 12,400 miles (20,000 km) of railroad track link Hokkaidō with Kyūshū. Air travel is cheap and there are numerous ferry services to Japan's many islands.

─────── Major highway

++++++ Railroad

✈ Major airport

Air and Water

Flying is the quickest way to travel in Japan. There are 70 local airports. Japan is the only country that uses jumbo jets for internal flights because so many people wish to travel by air. There are several international airports; Tokyo has two—Haneda and Narita. Most international flights land at Narita, which is located 37 miles (60 km) north of the city. An efficient train link—the Narita-Express—runs between Tokyo and Narita Airport. More airports are being built on artificial islands constructed along the Pacific coast to serve the largest cities.

In the past, people used ferries to travel between Japanese islands, but today ferries are used mainly to link the smaller islands. The country's merchant fleet is the third-largest in the world. Japan's main ports—Chiba, Kōbe, Nagoya, and Yokohama—all lie on the east coast of Honshū.

The Tokyo–Chitose (Hokkaidō) air route is the busiest in the world. Six million passengers fly this route every year.

Arts and Living

"Japan is a country that permits the harmonious existence of old and new. Japan's very existence and functioning have been built upon this harmony."

Japanese sociologist Kato Hidetoshi

Many of the things today considered typically "Japanese" have their origin in China. The ornate Japanese script, elegant silk clothes, refined literature, and Buddhist religion were all borrowed from the court of the Chinese emperors in about the sixth century. During the Heian period (A.D. 794–1185), however, Japan shook off the influence of China and began to build a rich and original culture that was all its own.

For centuries after, Japan was virtually a closed world. The traditional culture that developed was very formal. Elaborate rules governed everything from greeting acquaintances to writing poetry. Tradition and refinement were valued more highly than originality or self-expression. People thought of themselves less as individuals than as part of a society in which rules and duties were to be followed for the greater good.

Then, in the mid-19th century, Japan opened itself to the outside world. Its people enthusiastically adopted the technologies that came from the West—movies, trains, and factory machines—and in many cases, improved on them! Japanese culture nevertheless modernized without losing any of its originality. Today life in Japan is an often astonishing mix of the traditional and modern. Japanese cities blend red and gold temples with daring modern skyscrapers, and Japanese homes are likely to have both a state-of-the art computer and an abacus.

Japanese arts often have a spiritual quality. Rock ("flat") gardens such as this one at Tōfuku-ji Temple in Kyōto are designed to encourage meditation.

FACT FILE

- Japanese people do not wear shoes inside their homes. They leave their shoes outside and wear plastic slippers inside.

- Eighty-five percent of Japanese couples marry in a Shinto ceremony.

- The Japanese population is the longest-lived in the world. On average people in Japan live to 80 years of age.

- The Japanese spend over $4.6 billion per year on books. Only the United States and Germany spend more.

- According to a UN survey, the Japanese people have the sixth-best quality of life in the world.

THE ARTS

A succession of trips to China by envoys and students during the ancient period (A.D. 250–710) and the Nara period (A.D. 710–784) meant that early Japanese arts were influenced by those of China. Today many traditional crafts also have the status of art forms. Activities as diverse as garden design, paper folding, writing, flower-arranging, and even drinking tea are all "arts" in Japan and often have a spiritual dimension.

Architecture Old and New

In Japanese cities ancient and modern often exist side by side. Here the gabled, curving roofs of Ōsaka Castle contrast with the shiny twin office buildings behind.

Many of Japan's most beautiful buildings are its Buddhist temples and Shinto shrines. The earliest shrines were simply sacred places—a grove, rock, or pool, for example—that were separated from the surrounding land by a rope. Later the shrines became simple wooden-framed structures, guarded by a red, π-shaped gate, or *torii*. The main path to the shrine is often flanked by stone lionlike creatures called *komainu*.

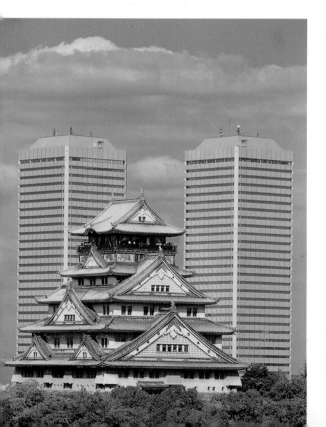

Because Buddhism came to Japan by way of China, traditional Buddhist temples were influenced by Chinese architecture. They have slender pillars and are painted in bright colors such as red and gold. Their tiled roofs have edges that sweep upward in pleasing curves. The temple often features a tower-like pagoda (*see* p. 99), which houses a relic—a tooth or bone, for example—of the Buddha.

Some modern Japanese architects echo the graceful lines of traditional architecture in new buildings. Kenzo Tange, one of Japan's most popular architects, designed the National Stadium in Tokyo and the Peace Center in Hiroshima. Traditional Japanese architecture has also influenced architects worldwide. For example, Robie House in Chicago, built by American architect Frank Lloyd Wright (1867–1959), has Japanese-style long, low balconies and roofs.

Buildings in Japan are sturdily constructed to withstand the shocks of small earthquakes that shake the country daily. Traditional houses are made of wood, a material flexible enough to bend with minor tremors. In cities, skyscrapers are built of steel and concrete but are also designed to sway in earthquakes, rather than topple and collapse. Most Japanese homes are small and rooms are created with movable partitions, or screens, that can be slid to one side to make living spaces larger or smaller.

Buddhist temples are built around a central compound and consist of several buildings.

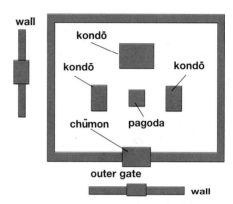

The main parts of a Buddhist temple are:

kondō or **hondō:** the main halls of the temple where the statues of the Buddha are placed.
pagoda: tiered, towerlike building that houses a relic of the Buddha.
kōdō: the lecture hall where the monks study and recite scriptures.
chūmon: the inner temple gate, often guarded by fierce-looking stone figures.

Sculpture: *Haniwa* and *Netsuke*

The earliest known sculptures are the clay statues known as *haniwa* that date from the Kofun period (A.D. 300–710). *Haniwa* are simple figures of warriors, servants, and animals that were placed in the burial mounds of chieftains, to honor or serve the lord (*see* p. 51).

After Buddhism reached Japan in the sixth century, sculptors produced works for Buddhist temples, using wood, clay, or bronze. One of the most famous is the Great Buddha of Kamakura, a giant bronze figure cast in the 13th century. Statues of Buddha or Buddhist priests had calm faces. Other figures, such as the Guardian Kings at Kamakura, are carved with ferocious, threatening faces to frighten away the enemies of Buddha.

At the other end of the scale from these massive sculptures are the tiny sculpted figures known as *netsuke* that date back to the 17th century. They are carved in minute detail in wood or ivory and were designed to be attached to a purse or a medicine box by a silken sash.

Hokusai: "The Old Man Mad About Drawing"

One of the very greatest wood-block artists was Katsushika Hokusai (1760–1849). Hokusai lived almost all his long life in Edo (Tokyo), where he began his career as a book illustrator.

In 1814 he began work on a series of *manga* (cartoon) sketchbooks in which he drew the bustling street life of Edo. In the *manga* are everyone from acrobats and musicians to geisha and samurai.

Later in life Hokusai turned his hand to producing bold, colorful views of Japan's beautiful landscapes. His most famous series of prints depicts Japan's holiest place—Mount Fuji. In his *Thirty-six Views of Mount Fuji*, Hokusai depicted its snow-capped cone from many vantage points (*see* p. 21). In the *Great Wave at Kanagawa*, the holy mountain is just visible in the trough of a giant breaking wave.

Hokusai produced an enormous amount of work—more than 30,000 prints, sketches, and paintings. He signed his work with many different signatures—changing his name more than 50 times. Hokusai appeared frequently among his names, but his favorite, adopted late in life, was a name meaning "old man mad about drawing."

Painting: "Images of the Floating World"

Early Japanese painting was also inspired by Buddhism and influenced by China. Between the 12th and 14th centuries, artists painted long picture scrolls that told the stories of heroic battles or ancient legends through a series of images that were "read" from right to left. Other artists painted wooden screens or drew witty caricatures—pictures that distort a person's features— that portrayed noblemen and officials as monkeys, frogs, and other animals.

From the 14th century, many artists, influenced by the Zen school of Buddhism, produced peaceful landscapes in ink wash (diluted ink powder). In the 17th century, colored wood-block prints became fashionable. The artist drew the original picture on transparent paper, which was then stuck onto a piece of cherrywood. The engraver then cut out the wood through the paper to make a woodblock for printing. A woodblock was cut for each color that had to be printed; sometimes up to ten separate blocks were used. Two famous wood-block artists were Andō Hiroshige (1797–1858) and Katsushika Hokusai (*see* box opposite).

Wood-block prints were cheap enough to be bought and enjoyed by ordinary people. They showed fleeting impressions of landscapes, beautiful women, or scenes from plays or legends. The wood-block tradition is called *ukiyo-e*, which means "images from the floating world." In the 19th century, the prints reached Europe, where they were much admired by artists such as Édouard Manet, Mary Cassatt, and Henri de Toulouse-Lautrec, who imitated their bold compositions and flat, pure colors in their own work.

The Japanese wood-block artists of the Edo period produced striking images of the natural world. This painting of a white heron landing on a pond edged by violet irises is by Andō Hiroshige—one of Japan's greatest artists.

Haiku

Haiku poems express brief and meaningful insights into nature or human life. The pioneer of the form was the poet Matsuo Basho (1644–1694). An artist as well as a poet, he traveled around Japan, visiting some of his country's more remote regions and composing poems about his impressions of the sights he saw.

The mood of many haiku is often thoughtful, but there can be moments of humor, too. Another poet, Kobayashi Issa (1763–1827), wrote the following well-known haiku:

For fleas, also, the night
Must be so very long,
So very lonely.

Slowly, slowly, climb
Up and up Mount Fuji
O snail.

Translations of haiku may have more syllables because it is not always possible to give the meaning in another language in only 17 syllables. Writing a short poem may seem simple, but why not try it and see if it is so easy?

Novels and *Haiku*

One of the earliest and most important works of Japanese literature is a long novel called *The Tale of Genji*. It was written in the early 11th century by a lady at the imperial court, Murasaki Shikibu (about 978–1014). Her novel tells of the travels and adventures of young Prince Genji. It was written in Japanese at a time when the language of the court was Chinese and only women and ordinary people spoke Japanese. Lady Murasaki also kept a diary, which gives intimate descriptions of life at the imperial court.

Lady Murasaki's novel contains lots of poetry—a favorite pursuit of the aristocracy of the period. Lady Murasaki would probably have known the *Manyoshu*, the first collection of Japanese poetry, compiled in around 750. The *Manyoshu* includes about 4,500 poems written mostly during the seventh and eighth centuries.

One of best-known forms of Japanese poetry is the *haiku* (*see* box). If you count the syllables in the Japanese words, you should find five syllables in the first line, seven in the second, and five in the third. Another traditional form is the *tanka*, which contains 31 syllables. Today there are poetry clubs in many Japanese towns and cities, where members practice writing *haiku* or *tanka*.

Japan also produced many fine novelists in the 20th century. One of the most talented, Mishima Yukio (1925–1970), committed suicide in the manner of the samurai to protest against the Westernization of Japan.

In traditional Japanese puppet theater— bunraku—the puppeteers make little attempt to hide themselves. They move the puppets so convincingly, however, that the audience is drawn into the play and almost forgets that the puppeteers are there.

Traditional Drama

Japanese theater has many traditional forms. *Nō* theater dates back to the 14th century. More than half the plays performed today were written by Zeami Motokiyo (1363–1443), his son, or his grandson. The plays proceed at a solemn and stately pace, with music and dancing. Actors wearing carved wooden masks take the roles of heroes or villains and act out stories from history or legend. Many of the lines are chanted by a chorus.

Often more than one *nō* play was performed at a sitting. In between these serious plays, maskless actors performed a kind of farce known as *kyōgen* to provide a lighthearted break for the audience.

Another form of theater, *kabuki*, first developed in the 17th century. The actors wear bold makeup and bright costumes and act in a lively, exaggerated style. *Kabuki* plots are dramatic tales of love, jealousy, loyalty, and revenge. The audience is swept along in the action, cheering the heroes and hissing at the villains. *Kabuki* is thought to have originated from the dances

The word *kabuki* is made up of three Japanese characters: "song" (*ka*), "dance" (*bu*), and "skill" (*ki*).

Many of Japan's traditional instruments derived from those played in neighboring China and Korea. The biwa, for example, was introduced from China in the seventh century.

that a shrine maiden from Izumo shrine, named Okuni, performed to raise money. Nevertheless, women are not allowed to act in *nō* or *kabuki* plays, so the female parts are played by men.

Bunraku, or puppet theater, dates from the same time as *kabuki*. A narrator tells the story, and puppets act out the plot. The largest puppets, which are two-thirds life-size, are operated by three puppeteers at once. The puppeteers dress in black and are hidden from the waist down by a screen. The puppet master, who has often trained for as long as 30 years, operates the puppet's head and right arm. Many of the best *bunraku* plays were written by Chikamatsu Monzaemon (1653–1724), often regarded as Japan's equivalent to English dramatist William Shakespeare.

Music Traditional and New

Many of the instruments and forms of traditional Japanese music were introduced from China in early times. At the emperor's court, small orchestras played a refined music called *gagaku*. Music often accompanied performances of *bunraku* and *kabuki* theater. During Buddhist and Shinto ceremonies, priests chanted or struck bells and drums.

Traditional instruments include the three-stringed *shamisen*, which has a long, unfretted neck and a rectangular or circular soundbox. The flat, 13-string *koto* is laid on the ground to be played with a pick and sounds like a harp. Another string instrument is the lutelike *biwa*. Flutes, drums, and gongs are also played. The *shakuhachi*, a bamboo flute, has a breathy, haunting sound. *Taiko* drumming is another traditional Japanese music that is still popular today at festivals and parades. The drums are very large, and the drummer needs lots of energy.

Today Western music forms are popular in Japan, including classical, rock, jazz, and pop. There are seven concert orchestras, based in Tokyo, Ōsaka, and Kyōto.

shō (mouth organ)

shamisen

biwa

Garden Design

Japan is celebrated for its landscape gardening. Unlike European and American gardens, Japanese gardens rarely feature grass lawns or flowers. Instead they are a meticulous arrangement of rocks, streams, trees, bushes, or sand, composed just like a painter composes color and shapes on a canvas. Even the landscape outside the garden plays a part in the composition of a Japanese garden—perhaps a distant mountain or a temple pagoda.

There are three main kinds of gardens. Tea gardens are created around teahouses (*see* p. 112). The trees and bushes of the tea garden are carefully clipped into shape. A path of stepping stones is laid through the garden, and there is a stone basin for guests arriving at the tea ceremony to wash their hands. At night the flickering light from a stone lantern adds to the atmosphere of peace and intimacy.

Hill gardens, mostly designed for private homes, are small parks with well-planned displays of flowering shrubs and small, artificial hills. The Jojuin Gardens at Kiyomizudera in Kyōto and Ritsurin Garden in Kumamoto, Kyūshū, are two of the best-known examples.

Flat gardens are quiet places for meditation, designed according to the principles of Zen Buddhism. They have few plants but feature flat areas of sand or gravel carefully raked into patterns, around rocks or pools that represent mountains, rivers, and oceans. The most famous flat garden is in Ryoan-ji Temple in Kyōto.

Japan's temples often stand in beautiful and tranquil gardens. They are places in which to stroll and meditate. This garden is at Rinno-ji Temple in Sendai, northern Honshū. The temple's pagoda rises above the well-tended shrubs and bushes, while carp swim in the peaceful pond. The Japanese associate the carp with strength and determination.

This intricate lacquerware box was made in the 19th century and was used to hold gloves.

Exquisite Crafts

Japan is famous for the beauty of its ceramics, silks, embroidery, lacquerware, and cloisonné (decorative enameling). Lacquerware are items such as bowls, trays, and boxes that are skillfully painted with lacquer, a varnish made from tree sap. Up to 50 steps are involved in lacquering even a simple bowl. Japan's fine metalwork, including armor, swords, and knives, has been renowned from ancient times.

Japan is also well known for its handmade patterned papers (*washi*). During the Heian period, people at court used *washi* to write poetry. Sometimes special papers were made to complement the style of a particular poem. Other traditional crafts, such as *origami* (paperfolding), *ikebana* (flower-arranging), and calligraphy, the art of beautiful writing with a brush pen, are popular leisure activities. *Origami* models are made by folding colored paper into shapes that can be as complicated as a flower. A favorite is to make an *origami* crane, which is a symbol of long life (*see* p. 44).

There are more than 20 different styles of arranging flowers. In fact *ikebana* does not always feature many flowers. It is more likely to be a careful arrangement of branches and leaves, positioned according to a set of rules. The finished arrangement represents Heaven, Earth, and humankind. An upward-pointing branch represents Heaven; one leaning to the right stands for humankind; and one leaning to the left indicates the Earth.

The Movies

Motion pictures were first shown in Japan in 1896; the first Japanese film was made in 1899.

Japan is a leading filmmaking nation. In the 1950s, movies featuring a monster called Godzilla, which were directed by Honda Ishiro (1911–1993), achieved cult status in the United States and Europe because of their special effects. A popular kind of movie in Japan was the adventure story dealing with the samurai. The *Seven Samurai*, a 1954 film by Kurosawa Akira (1910–1998), was later remade as the Hollywood western *The*

Magnificent Seven (1960). Another Kurosawa movie, *Yojimbo* (1961), became *A Fistful of Dollars* (1964), starring Clint Eastwood. Kurosawa's film *Ran* (1985) was his version of Shakespeare's play *King Lear*.

One of the greatest Japanese filmmakers was Ozu Yasujiro (1903–1963). Starting as an assistant cameraman at the age of 20, he went on to direct 54 films. Most of them were shot in a simple style, from a low viewpoint as if the camera was held by someone sitting on a traditional *tatami*-mat floor. This meant that Ozu had to make the unusual step of building ceilings on movie sets because they often appeared in shots. The films, which include his masterpiece, *Tokyo Story* (1953), tell the stories of the lives and problems of ordinary Japanese families.

Japanese animated films are also popular. One well-known movie, *Akira* (1987), by Otomo Katsuhiro, is based on *manga*, Japanese adult comic books that are often criticized for their violent content.

Two generations of a Japanese family sit down to drink tea and chat. The Japanese rarely use chairs but sit on cushions on the floor.

EVERYDAY LIFE

Family life in Japan has been transformed in the last hundred years. A century ago the vast majority of people lived in the countryside. Eldest sons typically followed their father's profession. Families were often large, with grandparents, parents, and their children, and sometimes uncles and their families, all living together under one roof. Most married couples had four children or more. Marriages were arranged by the couple's parents, helped by a matchmaker. When the eldest son married, his wife came to live with his family. Wives worked in the home almost like servants and obeyed their husbands in all things.

How to Say...

The Japanese language can seem very odd to English speakers (and vice versa!).
For example, Japanese has no words for "the" or "a," and there are no plural forms
of nouns (you may have noticed that in this book words like *haiku* or samurai are spelled
just the same whether there are one or many poems or warriors). Lots of Japanese words,
too, are pronounced the same but have different meanings; for example *hashi* can mean
both "chopsticks" and "bridge." What is more, Japanese is written with a system of
characters, or *kanji*, which can look bewildering to Western eyes (*see* p. 108).

The Japanese are very polite. Coworkers address each other, not by their first names
but with their family names, followed by "-*san*," which can stand for "Mr.," "Mrs.,"
"Ms.," or "Miss." Even friends use each other's surnames, but adding "-*chan*" for girls
and "-*kun*" instead of "-*san*." Japanese are especially courteous to people older than
themselves or to those who hold a more senior position—at work, for example.

Despite such difficulties, it is not hard to learn how to say some simple Japanese
phrases. A few are written below using the Roman alphabet, together with a rough
pronunciation guide. The vowels written with a bar (or macron) are pronounced just
the same as standard vowels but are held twice as long. A lengthened vowel can make
all the difference to the meaning of a word. For example, while *yuki* (without the
macron) means "snow," *yūki* (with the macron) means "bravery." For more help with
pronunciation, see p. 11.

Please   (when asking for something)
  o-negai shimasu (o-nengi she-
  ma-su)
Please (when offering something) *dōzo*
  (doo-zo)
Thank you *domō arigatō* (do-mohh
  ah-reeng-ah-tohh)
Yes *hai* (hi)   No *iie* (i-eh)
Good morning *o-hayō gozaimasu*
  (o-ha-yohh go-zigh-ma-su)
Good afternoon *konnichiwa*
  (kon-nee-chee-wa)
Good evening *kombanwa*
  (kom-ban-wa)
Goodbye *sayōnara* (sigh-yohh-na-la)

How are you? *o-genki desuka?*
  (oh-gen-kee deh-su-ka)
Sorry *gomen nasai* (go-men na-sigh)

Numbers:

One *ichi* (ee-chee)
Two *ni* (nee)
Three *san* (san)
Four *yon* (yon)
Five *go* (go)
Six *roku* (lo-ku)
Seven *nana* (na-na)
Eight *hachi* (ha-chee)
Nine *ku* (ku)
Ten *jū* (juhh)

Bowing

In Japan, people bow to greet one another or when apologizing. Bowing, or *ojigi*, takes the place of the Western custom of shaking hands.

It takes a long time to master the art of bowing. Mothers teach babies how to bow, and children continue to learn the rules of bowing at school. New company employees also spend time during their first weeks learning how to bow at work.

The depth of bow depends on the status of the person you are greeting. People bow at 15° to greet equals, a little farther forward at 30° to superiors, and a deep bow at 45° to apologize or greet very important people. The habit of bowing becomes so automatic that many people bow when speaking on the telephone. Many younger Japanese no longer bow and prefer to shake hands in formal situations, especially with foreigners.

These days, things are very different. Most sons now choose their own careers. The majority of people live in the city, where space inside houses is too cramped for grandparents to live with their relatives. Family units are much smaller: just a mother and father and one or two children. Marriages are no longer arranged, so people marry for love and shared interests. More married women now go out to work, though not usually when their children are young. On average, men marry aged about 28 and women at about 25.

The Japanese at Home

Japanese homes are small. The floors are covered with springy straw matting called *tatami*. No one wears shoes inside the house. People leave their outdoor shoes at the entrance and put on slippers instead. In the home, life goes on at ground level. Everyone sits on cushions on the floor. In winter, people warm themselves by sitting around a low table covered with quilts, with a heater underneath. At night, padded mattresses called *futon* are spread out on the floor for bedding. By day, the *futon* are packed away in closets so that the same room can double as a bedroom and living space.

The Japanese have used the metric system of measurement for decades. However, they still measure rooms in terms of the number of *tatami* (straw mats) that they will hold.

The Japanese have some of the best-equipped homes in the world. Almost all Japanese homes have a color televison, washing machine, and refrigerator.

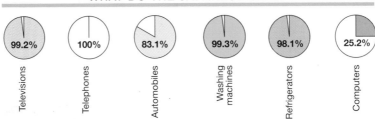

WHAT DO THE JAPANESE OWN?

99.2%	100%	83.1%	99.3%	98.1%	25.2%
Televisions	Telephones	Automobiles	Washing machines	Refrigerators	Computers

Source: Government of Japan, 1996

Most Japanese homes have many modern appliances, including a color television with cable and satellite channels, video recorder, stereo system, computer, and fax machine. There may be at least one Western-style room with a carpet, chairs, and a higher table. The main room of the house always has a traditional feature—a wall niche with a decorative scroll and flower arrangement.

In the evenings people enjoy a relaxing soak in a deep bath. They soap and rinse before getting in the tub because everyone shares the same piping-hot water.

Clothes—"Things Worn"

In everyday life, Western-style dress is very common. Businesspeople wear suits and leather shoes to work. At home and for informal occasions, most people wear casual clothes such as jeans or sweatsuits and sneakers. City people are more fashion conscious than those in country areas.

Traditional clothes are usually kept for special occasions. The *kimono* ("thing worn"), the traditional dress for both men and women, is a long, loose garment tied at the waist with a sash called an *obi*. Wooden clogs called *geta* or flat sandals called *zori* are worn on the feet. To wear with the V-shaped straps of the *geta* or *zori*, there are special socks called *tabi*. These are something like mittens for feet, with a section for the big toe split from the larger part for the other toes.

This elaborate embroidered coat was intended for wearing at court. The traditional clothes of today are usually much simpler.

Girls and women wear *kimono* for visiting shrines (*see* p. 111), and at coming-of-age ceremonies, graduations, weddings, and funerals. Boys and men can also wear *kimono* for ceremonial occasions but these are often in darker colors—blue or brown.

Uniforms play an important part in daily life. People working in department stores, factories, and offices in some large companies may wear uniforms.

Food and Drink

Rice is a staple food for Japanese people. In fact the Japanese word for "rice" also means "a meal." Rice is eaten at every meal and is usually boiled. It is also made into cakes, molded into cubes and patties, and even used to make the rice wine known as *sake*. Fish is the main form of protein. It is prepared in many different ways: broiled, deep-fried in batter with vegetables as *tempura*, or eaten raw. Several kinds of seaweed are eaten, too.

Sashimi are thin strips of raw fish. *Sushi* are rice patties seasoned with vinegar and topped with raw fish, seaweed, or vegetables. People sometimes dip the *sashimi* or *sushi* into a mixture of soy sauce and *wasabi*, a spicy radish paste, before eating them. Small pieces of pickled ginger also add to the flavor.

People traditionally ate little meat in Japan because it was against Buddhist principles, but times have changed. Meat is much more popular today, along with bread and dairy products. *Sukiyaki* is a dish made with thin slices of beef and chopped-up vegetables, all simmered in a soy and *sake* sauce.

Soybeans are another rich source of protein. Salty soy sauce is used to flavor food. Soybeans are also fermented and ground to make *miso* paste for soup, or

A chef puts the finishing touches on an elaborate dish. Japanese food is not only delicious, it should be beautiful to look at. The finest kind of Japanese food is known as kaiseki and is made from only vegetables and fish.

Japanese Green Tea

You can make Japanese green tea easily at home. A widely available green tea is called *bancha*, which is also very cheap. Boil 1 ½ pints of water. Meanwhile put 2 tablespoons of green tea leaves into a pot. When the water has boiled, carefully pour it over the tea leaves and leave it to steep for about two minutes.

Pour the tea into cups through a strainer. Don't add milk or sugar, as these will spoil the tea's delicate flavor.

In summer, the Japanese like to drink green tea cold. First they roast the green tea leaves in a pan for a few minutes, which gives the tea a delicious smoky flavor. Then they make the tea in the normal way, straining it and keeping it in the refrigerator.

made into blocks of curd called *tofu*. A filling winter dish called *oden* contains broiled and fried *tofu*, fish, cabbage, carrots, and other vegetables. Tea is the most popular drink. Alcoholic drinks include beer and *sake*.

Breakfast is a full meal, consisting of boiled rice, dried fish, seaweed, *miso* soup, and pickles. These days, some people prefer a Western-style breakfast of cereal, toast, and coffee. The midday meal is often a box lunch, or *bento*, containing rice, raw fish, and a little meat, pickle, and *tofu*. The evening meal consists of a wide variety of dishes, all served at the same time.

The Japanese version of fast food is noodles, made of different kinds of flour. *Soba*, made from buckwheat flour, are brown; *udon* are made from white flour. Noodles are often served in broth, with vegetables, shrimps, egg, or meat added. In summer, noodles are eaten chilled and topped with dried seaweed and a dipping sauce. When people are eating in a noodle bar, you may sometimes hear some loud slurping noises. It is not considered rude, just a way of showing you are enjoying the food. In hamburger restaurants there are regular burgers and some special dishes for Japan, such as *teriyaki* burgers flavored with soy sauce and octopus salad.

Japanese "candy" is very different from the sugar-based kind found in the West. It is often made from a sweet red-bean paste called *anko* and thick, sticky rice.

It is common to take guests out to eat at a restaurant rather than invite them home for dinner. Most restaurants serve only one kind of food, such as *sushi* or noodles. The presentation of each dish is very important—the food must be carefully arranged to look its very best and most appetizing (*see* p. 105).

One very unusual Japanese food item is the bony fish known as *fugu*, or puffer. It is a popular delicacy in restaurants. *Fugu* chefs are specially trained to remove all the parts of the fish that are poisonous. Each year, however, people still die from eating *fugu* that has not been correctly prepared.

Education

Schooling starts early in Japan. Many children attend preschool from the age of three. Formal schooling begins at six and is compulsory and free until the age of 15. Pupils spend six years at elementary school, followed by three years at junior high school. Most students then go on to study at a senior high school for another three years, to prepare for university or college training. There are more than 450 universities in Japan and 600 colleges.

Japanese children work very hard at school. Monday through Friday, school hours are 8:30 A.M. to 3:30 P.M. Children also go to school on Saturday mornings. At elementary and junior high school, much time is spent learning to read and write the difficult Japanese language (*see* p. 108). Many junior and senior high school students study English, too.

Throughout their school career, students face examinations. Some children take their first exam at three to get into the best preschools! Students must later pass exams each year. The entrance exams for colleges and universities are very difficult. Many pupils go to *juku*, or cramming schools, for extra classes that will help them to pass these exams. No wonder that this time of a student's life is known as "examination hell."

EDUCATIONAL ATTENDANCE

Further (university; 18+)   21.2%

Secondary (high school; 13–18)   96%

Primary (6–12)   100%

The chart above shows the percentage of Japanese who study at each of stage of schooling.

Learning Japanese

Japanese is a complicated language that takes many years to learn to write. It has three different scripts. The *kanji* script is used to convey basic words such as nouns and verbs.

The most important script uses characters called *kanji*. If you look at the *kanji* for rain (left), for example, you can almost see rain streaming from a rain cloud. Originally *kanji* came from China but over the years they changed their forms, and the Japanese invented new ones.

Simple *kanji* were used to build more complex ones. The *kanji* for "forest" (right), for example, is made up of the *kanji* for "tree," repeated three times. Similarly the *kanji* for "plumtree" (left) also contains the *kanji* for "tree." Japanese schoolchildren learn nearly 2,000 different *kanji*.

Another script, *hiragana*, is used to show the grammatical endings of words. A third script, *katakana*, which has 46 letters, is used for writing foreign words. Many foreign words are written using *katakana*—for example, *bijinesuman* (businessman) and *gorufu* (golf). Some borrowed words sound so different in Japanese that they are hard to recognize! If foreign words are too long, Japanese shorten them—for example *waapuro* (word processor).

A Healthy Nation

In Japan, people expect to live to a ripe old age. The average life expectancy—76 for men and 82 for women—is the highest in the world. This long life is partly due to the healthy Japanese diet.

The standard of health care is also high. Hospitals and doctors' offices use the latest medical equipment and there is good health education in schools and amongst the public. Health care is paid for by medical insurance. Sixty percent of this insurance is provided by private businesses, which cover the costs of their employees' treatment. Private medical insurance pays for the rest. Most doctors and hospitals in Japan use Western type medicine, but oriental medical techniques are also practiced.

Japan spends almost 7 percent of its gross national product (GNP) on health care—about half that spent on health care in the United States.

Sport and Leisure

Many different sports are played in Japan. One of the most popular is baseball, which was introduced from the United States in the late 19th century. Japanese baseball is called *yakyū*. *Yakyū* has different rules from the American game and is played on a smaller field. There are two national leagues—the Central and Pacific leagues. League games are shown on television in summer, and everyone follows the progress of their favorite teams.

Sumō, or Japanese wrestling, is the national game and probably the oldest sport in Japan. It began in the third century A.D., and the first contests were held at Shinto shrines. The referees still dress as Shinto priests. *Sumō* wrestlers, called *rikishi*, are large and powerful, some weighing more than 330 pounds (150 kg).

Each year some 800 wrestlers take part in eight tournaments. Tickets for the tournaments sell out quickly, but the contests are also shown on television. Champion wrestlers are rich and famous. A skilled wrestler named Chiyonofuji recently held the title of Grand Champion for ten years.

Sumō bouts take place in a circular ring called a dohyo. The loser is the first man to step outside the ring or touch the ground with any part of his body except his feet. The referee, dressed in ceremonial Shinto robes, makes sure the rules are followed.

HOW THE JAPANESE SPEND THEIR MONEY

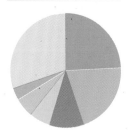

%

24.3 Food/drink/tobacco

20.5 Transport/communications

10 Entertainment/sports

6.2 Housing

5.5 Clothing

3.5 Health/medicine

30 Other

Source: Government of Japan

The Japanese spend most of their income on food and transport.

The Japanese love music. In 1996 they spent some $54 per head on tapes and CDs. Americans spend $40 per head.

Japan is well known for its martial arts. Most schoolchildren—girls as well as boys—learn at least one form of self-defense. These ancient sports developed from the fighting skills of samurai warriors. Practice begins with silent meditation to help focus the mind. *Judo*, meaning "the way of gentleness," *aikido* meaning "the way of spiritual harmony," and *karate*, meaning "empty hand," are all forms of unarmed combat. The traditional art of archery is called *kyudō*. *Kendō* is the art of fencing with bamboo staffs.

Gardening is one of the most popular leisure activities in Japan. Many homes have window boxes and a small yard about six feet square (0.6 sq. m). This tiny garden usually contains sand raked into patterns, a single tree, or a rock or two. Bonsai is the traditional art of growing miniature trees. Bonsai trees reach only 1 to 2 feet (30 to 60 cm) high. The trees are carefully pruned and wired to make sure the branches grow into a balanced shape. The oldest bonsai trees are more than 200 years old.

In their free time, the Japanese love to shop and go to the movies and concerts. They also enjoy playing *pachinko*, a pinball game. *Karaoke*, which involves singing along to recorded background music, always makes for a good night out. *Karaoke*, meaning "empty orchestra," has become popular in many other countries.

At home, Japanese people watch television or the latest film on video, practice a musical instrument, or listen to music. Reading is another relaxing activity. Besides books, there are about a hundred daily newspapers to choose from, and thousands of comics and magazines. After the United States and Germany, Japan has the third-highest book sales in the world.

Health clubs are visited throughout the year. For less active people, there are "mind gyms," where stressed businesspeople go to relax and listen to soothing music while they rest on chairs that sway gently. The Japanese are enthusiastic tourists, although work does not allow much time to take long vacations.

Religion Today

The Japanese are a deeply religious people. Ceremonies and rituals lie at the heart of their way of life.

Shinto is the most ancient Japanese religion (*see* p. 49). It has no scriptures like the Christian Bible or the Islamic Koran, giving rules about what is right and wrong. Instead, Shinto teaching emphasizes the importance of believers carrying out simple rituals to cleanse themselves and their things of "impurities." Shinto has no concept of sin in the Christian sense; people may become impure when they are ill or are in mourning, for example.

People visiting Shinto shrines purify themselves first before entering by rinsing their hands and mouths with water. At the shrine itself, people make an offering of a coin to the *kami*—the spirit of the shrine. On special occasions, gifts of food and drink are offered, or even a sacred dance or a *sumo* contest are held. Many people visit shrines to pray for good luck.

State Shinto

According to the Shinto religion, ancestors and famous figures from history are also gods. In the 1870s, the Japanese emperor established a national religion called State Shinto. It stressed patriotism, or love of country, and revered the Japanese emperor as a god. After World War II (1939–1945), the Allied victors outlawed State Shinto and made the emperor declare that he was not a god.

A Shinto priest adjusts the ceremonial robe of a young man.

The Tea Ceremony

Chanoyu is the tea ceremony, a ritual that aims to achieve a feeling of peace and harmony and to open the mind for meditation. It began among Buddhist monks in China. The Japanese "way of tea" was developed by the 16th-century Zen master, Sen no Rikyu. In addition to martial arts, samurai warriors studied the tea ceremony.

The ritual draws on both Buddhist and Shinto ideas. It takes place in a beautiful tea garden (*see* p. 99) and can last as long as four hours. At different points in the ceremony, guests admire the garden and the teahouse and discuss subjects such as nature, while their host prepares *cha* (green tea; *see* p. 106).

Guests sit Japanese style with their knees bent and their legs tucked under them. The bitter tea is served without sweetener in little cups. After the *cha* has been drunk, the guests admire the beauty of the cups and eat a sweet cake.

Tea masters, like the woman above, train for years to perfect the art of the *chanoyu*. All the objects used—kettle, tea bowls, serving ladle—are chosen especially for their beauty. Even preparing the tea has a set of rules, every move the tea master makes is important and has a meaning. The tea used is powdered green tea which is made frothy by using a bamboo whisk before serving.

Students pray for good exam results, and businesspeople pray for success at work.

Japan's most important Shinto shrine is at Ise, which lies in a remote area southeast of Nara and Ōsaka. The shrine is sacred to the Shinto sun goddess, Amaterasu (see box). For some 1,300 years, the shrine has been demolished and rebuilt every 20 years with fresh timber from the surrounding cypress woods.

Buddhism (see p. 52) is as important as Shinto. Most Japanese are both Shintoists and Buddhists and find no contradiction in following both religions. Two particularly popular schools of Buddhism in modern Japan are Zen and True Pure Land.

Zen is a branch of Buddhism that developed in medieval times. It emphasizes the practice of meditation and self-control as the way to inner peace. Zen Buddhism was taken up by samurai warriors (see p. 55), who practiced meditation to prepare for combat. The martial arts developed by the samurai express Zen ideas. Zen Buddhists also developed the tea ceremony (see p. 112) and the meditation garden.

True Pure Land was an offshoot of an earlier Buddhist sect (group) called Pure Land. True Pure Land teaches that ordinary people can find salvation through simple prayers that are sincerely made. Unlike monks who belong to other, more orthodox (mainstream) Buddhist sects, True Pure Land Monks may eat meat and get married.

Buddhist places of worship are called temples—called *tera* or *ji* in Japanese (see p. 93). The temples are filled with burning incense and the murmur of chants and prayers. Zen monks sit meditating on the ground cross-legged and with their wrists resting on their

Amaterasu

The most important god, or *kami*, in Shinto is the sun goddess, Amaterasu. According to legend Amaterasu's brother Susano-ō, who was in charge of the Earth, was jealous of his sister. He made such a noise in the Heavens that Amaterasu fled into a cave, plunging the world into darkness. The other gods coaxed her out of the cave by performing a comical dance with a spear and tempting her with a beautiful jewel and bronze mirror. As soon as the laughing Amaterasu left the cave, sunlight returned. Amaterasu's grandson Ninigi became the first ruler of Japan. The goddess gave Ninigi three gifts—a sword, mirror, and jewel—which became the special treasures of the imperial family.

Zen Buddhists also try to gain enlightenment by meditating on *kōan*, or riddles. The most famous *kōan* is "What is the sound of one hand clapping?"

knees. To stop them from falling asleep, they are occasionally struck with a bamboo stick.

Many Japanese people also follow the teachings of Confucius, a Chinese philosopher who lived about 500 B.C. Few Japanese follow the Christian religion. In cities, however, people sometimes celebrate weddings in a Western-style chapel.

Millions of people follow one of Japan's new religions, of which there are more than 200. Many of these new faiths contain elements of Shinto, Buddhism, or Christianity. A Buddhist sect called Sōka Gakkai ("Value Creation Society") is a popular new religion, with some 20 million members. Another sect called Aum Shinrikyō ("Supreme Truth") believed that the world was going to end in 1997. Aum Shinrikyō became notorious in 1995 when some of its followers released deadly nerve gas on the Tokyo subway. Twelve people died and some 5,500 others were injured in Japan's worst terrorist attack.

A Calendar of Festivals

The Japanese year contains many religious festivals, and there are 13 national holidays (*see* box opposite). One of the most important festivals in Japan is held at New Year and is called *Ganjitsu*. On New Year's Eve, the bells ring out to mark the end of the old year. Special decorations made of pine, bamboo, and plumtree branches are placed outside houses. During the New Year celebrations, which continue until January 3 or longer, people visit their families, eat special food, and play traditional games. Boys go kite-flying, while girls play a badminton-like game called *hanetsuki*. Many people pay a visit to a

Viewing Cherry Blossoms

During April, parties of office workers and families organize trips to local parks to view the cherry blossoms. Newspapers publish maps to show where the most beautiful blossoms can be found. A particularly popular place in Tokyo to view blossoms is Ueno Park. People picnic under the trees, and there is often music and dancing, too. The custom dates back to the reign of the emperor Saga (809–823).

Shinto shrine or Buddhist temple, and pray for health and happiness in the coming year.

March 3 is Girls' Day. Girls visit one another's homes to admire dolls dressed in beautiful *kimono*. The festival is also called Peach Day because the graceful flowers of this fruit are associated with girls. May brings Golden Week, when three festivals fall close together, and people have a chance to take a week off. At the end of Golden Week is Children's Day, formerly called Boys' Day, on May 5. Families with young sons fly paper streamers shaped like carp (*see* p. 99).

Summer festivals include *Tanabata*, the Star Festival, in July. The festival commemorates a princess and a farmhand who were in love but could meet only on one night a year. They are represented by two stars in the sky, the paths of which cross on this night. Children write wishes and tie them to bamboo branches.

National Holidays

January 1	New Year's Day
January 15	Coming of Age Day
February 11	National Foundation Day (*see* p. 47)
March 20 (or 21)	Coming of Spring Day
April 29	"Green" Day
May 3	Constitutional Memorial Day (*see* p. 71)
May 5	Children's Day Assumption Day
September 15	Respect-the-Aged Day (*see* p. 117)
September 23 (or 24)	Coming of Autumn Day
October 10	Health Sports Day
November 3	Culture Day
November 23	Labor Thanksgiving Day
December 23	The Emperor's Birthday (*see* p. 38)

At the Buddhist festival of *O Bon*, held in August or in some places in July, the spirits of the dead are thought to return to Earth. People go back to their home towns to visit the graves of their ancestors. They light bonfires and leave food on family graves to greet the spirits. People light lanterns and dance in the streets. August is also a popular month for moon-viewing. At night, small parties of people gather in gardens or on verandas to drink *sake* and read poetry.

Labor Thanksgiving Day (November 23) originally celebrated the harvest. Today, though, all workers are remembered on this day. The emperor traditionally makes an offering of *sake* to the gods.

The Future

"The Japanese are a great people. They cannot and should not be satisfied with a world role that limits them to making better radios and sewing machines..."

Singapore prime minister Lee Kwan

Japan has come a long way in the last 50 years. After World War II (1939–1945), Japan's economic recovery was so successful that it was hailed as an "economic miracle." In the late 1990s, however, Japan faced new difficulties, including a period of economic slowdown. There were other problems, such as overcrowding and an aging population. In the 21st century, Japan must tackle these problems, especially its financial troubles, if it is to keep its position as a world leader.

ECONOMIC DIFFICULTIES

The 1970s and 1980s were boom years for Japan's economy. Japanese companies grew and prospered and set up factories abroad. Japanese goods were sold worldwide, and the country built up a huge trade surplus. Japan's banks and financial institutions became the most powerful in the world.

By the 1990s, Japan's rapid growth was slowing. Japanese factories faced competition from other Asian countries, such as Taiwan and Korea, whose industries had also grown quickly. Around 1992 a period of slowdown began to affect countries all over the world. People in many countries had less money to spend on consumer goods, so there was less demand for Japanese products. Many Japanese businesses began to struggle. Some companies downsized part of their workforce; others were

Space is a valuable commodity in Japan's cities. The capital, Tokyo, has one of the most densely packed populations in the world.

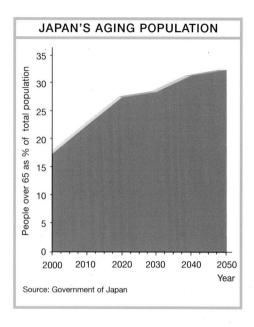

JAPAN'S AGING POPULATION

People over 65 as % of total population

Year

Source: Government of Japan

By 2050, experts predict that Japan's people over 65 will make up almost 35 percent of the total population.

forced to close entirely. The increased use of robots for routine and dangerous jobs in factories put more people out of work. For the first time in many years, unemployment began to rise.

Japan and several of its Asian neighbors entered a time of serious economic difficulty. The value of the Japanese currency fell. Some of Japan's financial institutions collapsed, and others looked less stable than they had for years. The situation also led to political upheaval, and new government leaders came and went.

In 1998, the government announced a series of measures aimed at supporting struggling businesses and boosting the economy. At the same time, the United States, European nations, and Japan tried to find ways of stabilizing world markets.

Over the next few years, Japan faces an uncertain economic future. What is certain, however, is that the hardworking Japanese are determined to find solutions to their problems. Because of its lack of natural resources, Japan will continue to depend on international trade and pioneer new developments in science and technology. Despite its present troubles, Japan will undoubtedly continue as a dominant force in world trade.

OVERCROWDING

At home, Japan faces the problem of overcrowding. Since the 1950s, cities and factories have grown so rapidly that in many areas, there is now a severe shortage of housing and lack of space.

Some city planners suggest that the answer to this problem is to build higher skyscrapers. This is possibly a dangerous solution in Japan because of the threat of earthquakes. Scientists believe that a major earthquake is now overdue and will strike the east coast of Japan's main island within the next few years. Many experts argue that it would be better to try and solve the problem of overcrowding by reclaiming more land from the sea for factories and new estates.

The government has also encouraged businesses to move away from cities into the countryside. Improvements in technology and communications mean that it is becoming easier for companies to relocate to rural areas and for people to run their businesses from home.

THE "SILVER GENERATION"

Japan also faces the prospect of an aging population. As health care improves, people can expect to live longer. At the same time, the birthrate has fallen, with married couples now having only one or two children. Smaller families mean that there will be fewer workers to help support a rising number of old people, known in Japan as "the silver generation." Japan is one of the first nations in the world to tackle this problem. With its customary resourcefulness, it is already seeking solutions.

An elderly woman sits reading beneath a cherrytree. Traditionally the Japanese have valued old age as a time of wisdom and contentment.

Almanac

POLITICAL

Country name:
Official form: Japan
Local official form: *Nippon/
Nihon*

Nationality:
noun: Japanese (singular and
plural)
adjective: Japanese

Official language: Japanese

Capital city: Tokyo

Type of government: parliamentary
democracy

Suffrage (voting rights): everyone 20
years and over

Independence: 660 B.C. (traditional)

National anthem: "Kimigayo" ("Our
Emperor's Reign")

National holiday: December 23
(Emperor's Birthday)

Flag:

GEOGRAPHICAL

Location: Eastern Asia; latitudes
30° to 45° north and
longitudes 127° to 146° east

Climate: Ranges from subtropical in
the south to cool temperate
in the north.

Total area: 145,835 square miles
(377,800 sq. km)
land: 99.2%
water: 0.8%

Coastline: 18,500 miles (29,800 km)

Terrain: mostly mountainous and
rugged

Highest point: Mount Fuji,
12,389 feet (3,776 m)
Lowest point: Hachiro-gata,
-13 feet (-4 m)

Natural resources: fish

Land use (1993 est.):
forests and woodland: 68%
arable land: 12%
permanent pastures: 2%
other: 18%

Natural hazards: volcanoes and
earthquakes

POPULATION

Population (1999 est.): 126,182,077

Population growth rate (1999 est.):
0.2%

Birthrate (1999 est.): 10.48 births
per 1,000 of the population

Death rate (1999 est.): 8.12 deaths
per 1,000 of the population

Sex ratio (1999 est.): 96 males per
100 females

Total fertility rate (1999 est.): 148
children born for every 100
women in the population

Infant mortality rate (1999 est.):
4.07 deaths per 1,000 live births

Life expectancy at birth (1997 est.):
total population: 80.11 years
male: 77.02 years
female: 83.35 years
Literacy:
total population: 99%
male: 99%
female: 99%

ECONOMY

Currency: yen (¥); 1¥ = 100 sen

Exchange rate (1999):
$1 = 110¥

Gross national product (1998):
$2.903 trillion (second-largest
economy in the world)

Gross national product by sectors:
agriculture: 1.9%
industry: 38%
service: 60.1%

Average annual growth rate
(1990–1996): 1.4%

GNP per capita (1998 est.): $23,100

Average annual inflation rate
(1990–1997): 1.5%

Unemployment rate (1998): 4.4%

Exports (1996): $410.9 billion
Imports (1996): $349.1 billion

Foreign aid given (1999): $9.1 billion

Human Development Index
(an index scaled from 0 to 100 combining statistics
indicating adult literacy, years of schooling, life
expectancy, and income levels):
94.0 (U.S. 94.2)

TIME LINE—JAPAN

World History	**Japanese History**

c. 10,000 B.C.

c. **10,000** Invention of bow and arrow.

c. **6000** Rice cultivation starts in Asia.

c. **10,000** Start of the Jōmon culture.

c. **7000** The world's earliest surviving pottery is made.

1151 First use of explosives in war by China.

1099 The First Crusade captures Jerusalem.

1066 Normans conquer England.

1192 Minamoto Yoritomo bcomes the first shogun (military dictator) of Japan. The emperor becomes a figurehead, without real power.

1002 Lady Murasaki completes *The Tales of Genji.*

c. 1000

c. 700 B.C.

551 Birth of the Chinese thinker Confucius.

c. **563** Birth of the Buddha.

221–207 The reign of Qin Shihuangdi, the first emperor of China.

c. **300** Start of the Yayoi period; rice cultivation, metalworking, and the potter's wheel are introduced from China and Korea.

982 Greenland discovered by Eric the Red.

800 Charlemagne is crowned emperor of Western (Holy) Roman Empire.

838 Contacts between China and Japan end.

794 Heian-kyō (Kyōto) becomes the capital.

760 The first great anthology of Japanese poetry —the *Manyoshu*— is collected.

710–784 Nara is briefly Japan's imperial capital.

681 Date of Japan's oldest historical document, the *Kojiki* ("The Record of Ancient Matters").

c. A.D. 300

330 Constantinople becomes capital of the Eastern Roman (Byzantine) empire.

589–618 The Sui dynasty of emperors reforms China and restores the Great Wall.

c. **350** Japan is unified under the Yamato clan.

c. **552** Buddhism is introduced from Korea.

592 Prince Shōtoku introduces a legal code and the Chinese calendar.

639 Muslim armies conquer the southern territories of the Byzantine empire.

618–907 China has a "golden age" of art and literature under the Tang dynasty.

c. 600

c. 1200

1215 The Chinese capital, Beijing, falls to the Mongol leader Genghis Khan.

1325 Foundation of the Aztec city of Tenochtitlán in Mexico.

1368 Foundation of the Ming dynasty in China.

1453 Turks capture Constantinople.

1492 Columbus lands in America.

1775–1783 American War of Independence.

1274 and 1281 Mongol forces twice invade Japan but are repelled with the help of *kamikaze* ("divine winds").

1467 Long period of civil war begins.

1542–1543 The Portuguese become the first Europeans to visit Japan.

1603 Beginning of the peaceful Edo period.

1635 Japan isolates itself from the rest of the world.

2000 The West celebrates the Millennium—2,000 years since the birth of Christ.

1993 Democrat Bill Clinton becomes U.S. president.

1989 Communism collapses in eastern Europe.

1963–1975 Vietnam War

1950–1953 Korean War

1995 Kōbe earthquake kills more than 5,000.

1992 Recession hits economy.

1989 Emperor Hirohito dies.

c. **1960** Japanese economy booms.

1956 Japan becomes a member of the United Nations (UN).

1947 Japan adopts a new Constitution.

c. 1945

c. 1800

1815 French emperor Napoleon is defeated at Waterloo.

1839–1860 The Opium Wars between China and Britain; China forced to make huge trading concessions.

1861–1865 American Civil War

1853 U.S. Commodore Matthew Perry forces first trading treaty with Japan.

1868 The Meiji Restoration—the shogunate is abolished and the emperor is restored to power.

1895 Japan defeats China in war over Korea.

1949 Communists take power in China.

1939–1945 World War II

1933 Adolf Hitler becomes German chancellor.

1914–1918 World War I

1911 Imperial rule ends in China.

1945 The United States drops atomic bombs on Hiroshima and Nagasaki; Japan surrenders.

1941 Japan bombs Pearl Harbor, bringing the United States into World War II.

1937 Japan launches invasion of China.

1905 Japan defeats Russia.

c. 1900

Glossary

Abbreviation:
Jp. = Japanese

Ainu: People thought
to be among the earliest
inhabitants of Japan.
ally: A country linked to
another by a treaty or league.
atomic bomb: Extremely
powerful bomb that uses
the energy released when the
nucleus of an atom is split.

Buddhism: Religion founded
by Siddhartha Gautama
(the Buddha; about 563–483)
that spread throughout central
and eastern Asia.
bullet trains (Jp. *shinkansen*):
High-speed Japanese trains.
bunraku **(Jp.):** Traditional
Japanese puppet theater.

ceremonial head of state:
A person, such as a king
or queen, who represents a
nation but holds no real power.
chihō **(Jp.):** The name for any
one of the nine regions of
Japan, for example Shikoku.
coalition: An alliance
between two or more
different political groups.
conservative: A political
philosophy based on main-
taining tradition and stability.
constitution: The fundamental
principles that underlie the
government of a country.
consumer goods:
Manufactured goods ready for
sale directly to the public—for
example, automobiles.

democracy: A process
that allows the people
of a country to govern
themselves, usually by voting
for a leader or leaders.
depression: An extended
slowdown in business
activity, during which
buying and selling decline
and unemployment rises.

Edo period, the: A peaceful
period (1603 to 1868)
in Japanese history when
the country was ruled
from Edo (later Tokyo)
by the Tokugawa family.
exports: Goods sold by
one country to another.

gross national product (GNP):
Total value of goods and
services produced by the
people of a country during
a period, usually a year.

haiku **(Jp.):** A form of
Japanese poetry made up
of three lines and 17 syllables.
Heian period, the: A period
(794–1185) in Japanese
history during which the
imperial capital was at
Heian-kyō (now Kyōto).

imports: Goods bought by
one country from another.
industrial(ized) nation:
A country where manufacture
is usually carried out with the
help of machinery.
inflation: The annual rate
at which prices increase.

Jōmon (Jp. "cord marked"):
Name given to the culture
of early inhabitants
of Japan whose pottery was
characterized by cord marks.

kabuki **(Jp.):** Colorful and
lively form of Japanese drama
dating from the late 1600s.
kamikazi **(Jp. "divine wind"):**
Term first used to refer to
the typhoon that hindered
a Mongol invasion in 1281.
In World War II, the term
referred to Japanese pilots
who flew suicide missions.
kanji **(Jp.):** Characters that
represent a word or part of
a word in written Japanese.
ken **(Jp. "prefecture"):**
The largest unit of local
government in Japan.
kimono **(Jp.):** Traditional
Japanese garment worn
by both men and women,
especially during festivals.

landscape gardening:
The creation of carefully
designed gardens where
land is developed for
human use and enjoyment.

Nara period: A period (710–
784) in Japanese history
during which the imperial
capital was based at Nara.
nationalism: People's sense
of belonging to a nation; also
the belief that a nation
should be independent of,
and sometimes superior to,
other nations.

natural resources: Products and features of the Earth that support life or satisfy people's needs.

nō (**Jp.**): Oldest form of Japanese drama, developed in the 1300s; characterized by formal gestures and tragic subject matter.

origami (**Jp.**): The art of folding paper into decorative objects.

pagoda: Tower often found in Buddhist temples.

pilgrimage: A religious journey to a shrine or holy place.

Shinto (Jp. "the way of the gods"): The oldest surviving religion of Japan, characterized by belief in nature spirits and the importance of ritual purity.

shogun (**Jp. "great general"**): Title given to the most powerful of the Japanese warlords.

sumō (**Jp.**): Japanese form of wrestling.

sushi (**Jp.**): A popular Japanese dish consisting of elaborately prepared raw fish, rice, and vegetables.

trade surplus: The amount of money earned by a country from exports after the cost of imports has been taken away.

Zen Buddhism: A school of Buddhism that teaches that the materials for meditation are found in everyday life.

Bibliography

Major Sources Used for This Book

Joseph, J. *The Japanese*. Harmondsworth, U.K.: Penguin, 1994.

Kanagawa, D. W., and J. Huey Erickson. *Japan for Kids*. Tokyo, Japan: Kodansha, 1992.

Sanson, G.B. *Japan: A Short Cultural History*. Stanford, CA: Stanford University Press, 1986.

Seidensticker, E. *Low City, High City*. Cambridge, MA: Harvard University Press, 1991.

Storry, R. *A History of Modern Japan*. Harmondsworth, U.K.: Penguin, 1990.

Tasker, P. *Inside Japan*. Harmondsworth, U.K.: Penguin, 1990.

General Further Reading

Clawson, E. *Activities and Investigations in Economics*. Reading, MA: Addison-Wesley, 1994.

The DK Geography of the World. New York: Dorling Kindersley, 1996.

The Kingfisher History Encyclopedia. New York: Kingfisher, 1999.

Martell, H.M. *The Kingfisher Book of the Ancient World*. New York: Kingfisher, 1995.

Further Reading About Japan

Grant, R.G. *Hiroshima and Nagasaki*. New Perspectives. Austin, TX: Raintree Steck-Vaughn, 1998.

Hartz, P. *Shinto*. World Religions. New York: Facts on File, 1997.

Herr, M., and M. Bartok. *Ancient Japan*. Ancient and Living Cultures. Glenview, IL: Goodyear Books, 1992.

Pilbeam, M. *Japan Under the Shoguns*. Looking Back. Austin, TX: Raintree Steck-Vaughn, 1999.

Snodgrass, M. E. *Japan and the United States: Economic Competitors*. Headliners. Brookfield, CT: Millbrook Press, 1993.

Some Websites About Japan

www.jinjapan.org

www.kids-japan.com

Index

Acknowledgments

Cover Photo Credits
Corbis: John and Dallas Heaton (Mount Fuji); John Dakers (Shinto priest dessing young man)

Photo Credits
AKG London: 50, 53, 95, 100; **Art Archive:** 33, 46, 67, British Museum 59; National Museum of Tokyo 51; Postal Museum Frankfurt 60; Victoria and Albert Museum 104; **Corbis:** 66; Yann Arthus-Bertrand 37; Bettmann 62; Burstein Collection 21, 94; Lloyd Cluff 16; John Dakers: Eye Ubiquitous 111; Jack Fields 119; John and Dallas Heaton 6; Robert Holmes 23, 90; Hulton-Deutsch Collection 64; Stephanie Maze 101; George McCarthy 30; Charles O'Rear 116; The Purcell Team 25, 71; Roger Ressmeyer 14, 31; David

Samuel Robbins 24, 44; Jeffrey L. Rotman 80; Royal Ontario Museum 49; Michael S. Yamashita 12, 19, 22, 26, 29, 36, 43, 68, 74, 77, 86, 88, 97, 109, 112; **Mary Evans Picture Library:** 98; **Rex Features:** 73; **Tony Stone Images:** 38, 92, Chad Ehlers 84, Charles Gupton 82, 105, Rich Iwasaki 39, Paolo Negri 40, Joel Rogers 99, Pete Seaward 87; **TRH Pictures:** US Army 63; **Werner Forman Archive:** Burke Collection New York 57, L. J. Anderson Collection 55.

Text Credit
The publisher would like to thank Alfred A Knopf, a Division of Random House Inc, for permission to reprint the extract on pp. 66–67 from John Hersey's *Hiroshima*.